The Edwardian Age

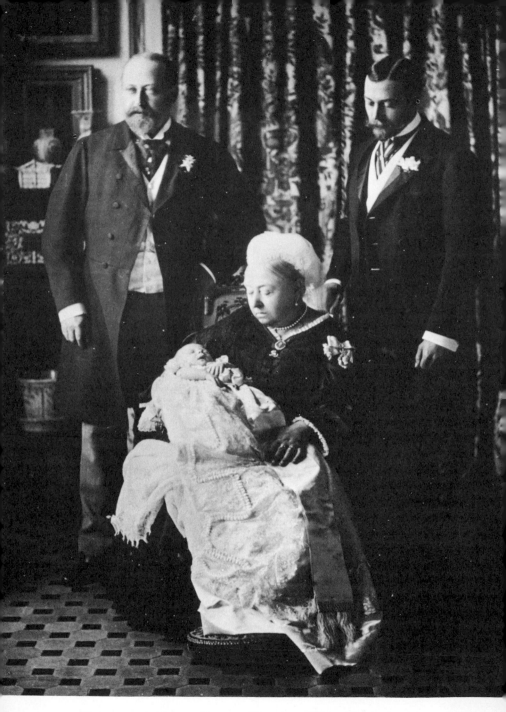

Four generations. Queen Victoria, King Edward the Seventh, King George the Fifth, and the infant King Edward the Eighth, later Duke of Windsor

The Edwardian Age

R. J. MINNEY

WITH ILLUSTRATIONS

LITTLE, BROWN AND COMPANY · BOSTON · TORONTO

Contents

Illustrations

King Edward shooting at Sandringham*
Mrs Alice Keppel*
The Countess of Warwick*
An Edwardian supper (*Courtesy of the* Illustrated London News)
A West End shop window in the Edwardian Age*
Prince Edward at a fancy dress ball at Devonshire House, 1897*
Princess Victoria and Princess Maud paddling. Photographed by their mother, Princess Alexandra (*Courtesy of the Gernsheim Collection*)
A house party at Windsor Castle, 1907*
Discussing the *Entente Cordiale*. King Edward and President Loubet of France. From a contemporary drawing*

following page 128

A group of Edwardian chorus girls—the Gibson Girls*
Vesta Tilley*
Edna May, the great Edwardian star of musical comedy*
Mrs Emmeline Pankhurst, being borne away by the police*
Mrs Pankhurst and her daughter Christabel in their prison clothes*
Kaiser Wilhelm the Second of Germany*
Prince Edward in a 12 horse-power Daimler with the future Lord Montagu of Beaulieu, July 1899*
Ballooning at Ranelagh, 1906*
Marconi, pioneer of wireless (*Courtesy of the* Illustrated London News)
King Edward with the American aviator Wilbur Wright at the aerodrome at Pau, 1909 (*Courtesy of the Mansell Collection*)
Winston Churchill as a young Cabinet Minister (*Courtesy of the* Illustrated London News)
Sandringham in 1891 (*Courtesy of the Mansell Collection*)
Prince Edward and Princess Alexandra with Alexandra's sister Dagmar, the Dowager Empress of Russia*

Courtesy of the Radio Times Hulton Picture Library

The Edwardian Age

Foreword

This is the portrait of an age and of the man who gave his name to that age. It was a brief age, spanning little more than nine years, but the impress of his personality was so powerful and the changes within that narrow span so varied and enduring that it has attained an honourable place alongside the goliath age of Victoria which preceded it and lasted close on sixty-four years.

It was fortuitous, yet convenient, that the transition between one age and the next should have occurred at almost the exact point when one century ended and the other began. Evolution is not, of course, achieved overnight. The process is long and slow, and the progress that distinguishes the age of Edward the Seventh and is still bearing a stupendous harvest in our own time—aviation, wireless communication, the cinema, motoring, and much more: all these had their beginnings in the preceding years, but it was in the Edwardian age that they came to notable fruition.

Thus at the end of nineteen centuries of the Christian era there occurred a series of dramatic developments which substantially altered the way of life of the peoples of the civilised world and eventually of the world as a whole. The horse, for thousands of years the chief means of land transport for both man and freight, gave place to the internal combustion engine, which in turn made transport possible by air.

Communication by wireless brought with it all the diversional possibilities of radio and in due course of television. The cinema with moving pictures and eventually the reproduction of human voices, supplied a varied portrayal of human activity, instructive as well as diverting. Electricity came into ampler use, replacing the naphtha flares of the markets and the dim gas-lighting of the city streets, and soon neon signs were flashing from the roof tops.

The ornamented *fin de siècle* decadence of Aubrey Beardsley and Oscar Wilde was succeeded by a creative richness and variety. It was for literature a wonderful landmark. A great host of talented writers such as H. G. Wells and Bernard Shaw, W. H. Hudson, Arnold Bennett and Saki, Maurice Hewlett and Laurence Housman enlivened the scene with their vivid and often amusing mosaics of that short fleeting age.

It is the purpose of this book to recapture the elegance and splendour of those glittering years—the opulence, the long week-ends of gaiety in magnificent country houses, the receptions, the balls and garden parties—a frenzied, flamboyant assertion of freedom after the long, severe, puritanical restraints of the reign of Queen Victoria.

Beneath that sparkling surface there was an abundant leaven. The national conscience was in ferment and expressed itself in legislation that ushered in the Welfare State. Women too were on the march. They were tired of emerging faintly scented from their boudoirs, swooning when a man got down on his knees and revived only with smelling salts. They sought an equal place beside the men. So far prostitutes, Florence Nightingale, some governesses and the Queen had found an outlet, and the few who were adventurous and accomplished astonishing feats of endurance in the deserts of the Near East, often mingled with passionate ardour, roused only scandal. In this Edwardian era they came out with their banners, chained themselves to the railings of 10 Downing Street and courted arrest and imprisonment to claim a voice in the councils of the nation—which eventually they won.

The King himself used his role of gay boulevardier to serve a worthier end. In his extensive travels, linked as he was by close family ties with the heads of States, he applied his influence and his unrivalled knowledge of affairs to the great advantage of his ministers and the nation. Few among his countrymen were as deeply aware of the lurking danger of war, and he strove by a balance of alliances to prevent the destruction of the way of life he so loved. His achievement was considerable. Working as a secret diplomatic agent during his seemingly frivolous excursions to Paris, Berlin and St Petersburg, he tried first to form an alliance with his nephew the Kaiser; when that failed he turned to France and it was through his personal initiative that the *Entente Cordiale* was he achieved in 1904, and extended to include Russia in 1908.

The praise of a contemporary statesman, Sir William Harcourt, who described Edward the Seventh as the greatest King since William the Conquerer, may appear extravagant; but of his greatness and his unique place in history there can be no doubt.

CHAPTER 1

The End of Victorianism

The Edwardian Age began at 6.30 on the evening of Tuesday, 22nd January 1901, for that was when Queen Victoria died, within a few months of her eighty-second birthday. Her grandson, Kaiser Wilhelm II of Germany, always claimed that she died in his arms. She did.

The official milestone from which the new age must be measured is set at that point; but King Edward's personality being powerful and pervasive, it had its roots far back in the nineteenth century and was known, by his own extensive social set as well as by the public, to have been in existence for a full forty years, though very thinly concealed under the strait-laced Victorianism of his mother. The old Queen knew of it, of course, and had been greatly troubled by his irregular tendencies during his maturing years: for she had tried together with her husband most resolutely to curb and mould the vagaries which both realised sprang from the unfortunate strains derived from his dissolute predecessors, the earlier Georges and in particular the Prince Regent and his promiscuous brothers.

The Queen's health had been failing for some months and the approaching end had brought members of her family repeatedly to her bedside at Osborne in the Isle of Wight, only to disperse when her strength rallied. Since the preceding February, that is to say for a full eleven months, her doctor kept giving strict instructions that bad news should be kept from her, and her secretaries scrutinised most carefully the telegrams bringing discouraging reports of the South African war. But by the middle of January 1901 it was clear that she could not hold out much longer. Yet again the family was assembled. The Prince of Wales, soon to succeed as King Edward the Seventh, arrived by special train from London, followed by the Princess of Wales and their son the Duke of York, later King George the Fifth; next came the German Kaiser, the Queen's grandson. The house was soon full to overflowing. Bedrooms had to be found for their suites in nearby houses and arrangements had to be made for feeding such a large number of people and assembling carriages to convey them to and from Osborne House.

The arrival of the Kaiser, who had not been invited, was strongly resented by the rest of the Royal family. He said, in his impeccable English: 'My first wish is not to be in the light, and I will return to London if you wish. I should like to see Grandmamma before she dies, but if that is impossible I shall quite understand.'[1]* As the end approached the Kaiser knelt by her bed and put his arm around her waist to support her. He kept it there for a full two and a half hours without stirring or wearying. The Prince and Princess of Wales and the Queen's daughters, Princess Helena, Princess Louise and Princess Beatrice, stood around the bed. The Duke of Argyll, the Queen's son-in-law (he was married to Princess Louise), likened her passing to the sinking of a great three-decker ship, for she kept rallying, then sinking.[1]

The awaited news was received by the nation with something akin to an emotional shock.[2] Only the very aged, those in their seventies and eighties, could remember a time when this legendary figure was not on the throne. It marked for them the passing of an age, for she had ruled the country for sixty-four years, and they recalled the

* Numerical references in the text refer to the Bibliography at the end of the book.

outbursts of loyalty and joy at her recent Jubilee celebrations. The widespread feeling was of sadness and awe. Forgotten were the criticisms of her aloofness for forty long years. Only her intense love of the country, her patriotic fervour and her greatness were remembered. The longest reign in English history had ended and many, wondering what the new reign would be like, told themselves that nothing would ever be the same again. Henry James said: 'We feel motherless today. We are to have no more of little mysterious Victoria, but instead fat, vulgar dreadful Edward.'

There were indeed grave misgivings about the new King. The public knew him as a stout, bearded playboy, now in his sixtieth year, who had frivolously frittered away his time on going to race-meetings, playing cards, spending his evenings with pretty women at the theatre and at supper, popping up at various gay resorts on the Continent and being involved in a succession of scandals. There had in fact been three public scandals, but gossip was rife as to how many more had been hushed up. That these had caused the utmost distress to the ageing Queen was well known, since it was only too apparent that in his behaviour and his way of life the new King was the very antithesis of his mother. These misgivings were shared by some of his own close friends, who viewed with anxiety the new King's capability and powers of self-discipline for the tasks that lay ahead: they knew how heavy and exacting those tasks were and had seen the formidable collection of official boxes requiring the Queen's attention even during the last week of her illness. Throughout his long heir-apparency, the longest in English history, Edward the Seventh had been denied by his mother both experience and information about State affairs. There was thus little with which he could have occupied his time and energy other than the diversions which now gave rise to so much doubt and despair.

In the churches many sermons voiced these gloomy forebodings and the congregations were asked to pray that the new monarch be steadied and strengthened by his responsibilities. *The Times,* in a leading article on the day following the Queen's death, declared bluntly: 'We shall not pretend that there is nothing in his long career which those who respect and admire him could wish otherwise.' Would there be a return to the profligacy that had brought the monarchy to such disrepute in the time of the Georges, which only the strength of character and high moral purpose of Victoria had succeeded in restoring to its full dignity? That barrier had at last been removed; the new King's activities could now enjoy their fullest expression; there was no longer any need for him to exercise even the scant restraint in order not to embarrass his mother—not, it was said with a sniff, that it had ever restrained him much.

CHAPTER 2

The King Asserts Himself

It must not be supposed that the country as a whole shared the views expressed from the pulpits and in *The Times*. Among the people, as Prince of Wales, the new King had enjoyed an immense popularity. His radiant charm, his winning smile conveyed, even as he drove by in a landau, a warmth and fellow-feeling that brought him close to them. He seemed to be the happiest man in the world and it would not have surprised many that he was, for, much though they revered his mother, they had not much in common with her. His father they disliked, not that there was much to dislike in him, but he was a German and for all his efforts at amiability, his manner appeared to them to be stuffy; and they were glad that his son had resisted the prolonged and exacting efforts to make him equally German and stuffy. Their sympathies accordingly were with the Prince, not because he was openly rebellious or even defiant, but because with every effort at discretion, he had gone his own way, which happened to be very much their way, for they too had human weaknesses of which they felt no need to be ashamed, however much some of their elders or neighbours might disapprove. They felt there was no harm in having a flutter on a horse or enjoying a game of cards or even in taking a pretty girl out to dinner. After all as a Prince he had the right to live in their dream world and many wished they had the means to do it too.

If they had any forebodings as to his ability to shoulder the burdens of kingship they readily shrugged them off, confident that his ministers were fully capable of coping with them—wasn't it for that that they had been voted into office?

But his accession brought in fact a change in Edward that few had expected. He was by no means prepared to drift with the tide and leave the decisions to others. From the outset he made it clear that he intended to be King, not along the pattern set by his mother, but on one of his own making.

On the morning after Queen Victoria's death the King left Osborne and travelled up to London by train in order to attend a meeting of the Privy Council at St James's Palace and take the oath as the new Sovereign.

At the time of his birth Lord Melbourne had suggested that the child should be christened Edward, after the Queen's father, the Duke of Kent, and also because it was a name that had already been used by English kings. But the Queen insisted that the boy's first name should be Albert. 'I *hope* and *pray*,' she wrote to her uncle King Leopold of Belgium, 'he may be like his dearest Papa.' Edward, she conceded, could be his second name. A quarter of a century later the Queen specifically indicated in a letter to her son what name he should use as King. 'It would be *impossible*,' she wrote with the emphasis of her *italics*, 'for you to *drop* your Father's. It would be *monstrous*, and *Albert alone* would *not do* . . . as there can be only *one Albert*.'[2] It was thus clearly her wish that he should be known as King Albert Edward the First.

It was a form that had been established and accepted in Germany, but which clearly he did not like, for now, as he took the oath and the Privy Councillors waited to learn what his choice would be, he announced, after a moving tribute to his mother, during which he nearly broke down: 'I have resolved to be known by the name of Edward, which has been borne by six of my ancestors.'[5]

This decisiveness, at the very commencement of the reign,

made a deep impression on those around him: it indicated a resolution and a sense of firmness that were to be in evidence throughout the reign.

A further example of this came a few days later. Queen Victoria had expressed the wish for a military funeral. After lying in state for ten days at Osborne, her body was placed in a coffin covered with a white pall and surmounted by the crown, the orb and the sceptre. It was then put onto a gun-carriage, which the King, the German Emperor and the other mourners followed on foot to East Cowes, where it was transferred to the royal yacht *Alberta*. As it was borne along the Solent through the long impressive avenue formed by battleships and cruisers, their flags flying at half-mast, a last solemn salute was fired in her honour. The wintry sky was only thinly veiled by mist and the setting sun, hanging low, shone dully red through it.

The King, following in the *Victoria and Albert*, noticed that the Royal Standard on his yacht was at half-mast. He asked why. 'The Queen is dead, Sir,' the Captain explained. 'But the King of England lives,' the King snapped and ordered the startled Captain to run the Royal Standard to the full height of the mast.

Shortly afterwards he exercised his authority in yet another direction. Queen Victoria had been greatly attached to both Osborne and Balmoral, and had more than once expressed the wish that these two houses, because of the cherished memories of her life in them with Prince Albert, should always remain in the possession of the British Crown.

The King decided to keep Balmoral because he felt that a residence in Scotland was necessary for the monarch; it offered him moreover many sporting advantages. But Osborne House he did not want. With Buckingham Palace and Windsor Castle as state residences and Balmoral as well as Sandringham, a vast estate which he had himself purchased for £220,000, as his personal homes, it seemed a heavy burden on the royal exchequer to maintain in addition a fifth estate. Osborne was by no means small: there were in fact 2,000 acres, which had been adorned by Prince Albert with a long, unattractive avenue of monkey-puzzle trees. After its purchase in 1843, the Queen demolished the house and had a large mansion built for her own use; to this a huge wing had been added for the accommodation of guests and servants, and a somewhat smaller wing as a residence for her daughter Princess Beatrice (the widow of Prince Henry of Battenberg) and her family. The King could not see what use he could make of it. After discussing it with his heir, later King George the Fifth, who did not want it either, King Edward made a gift of Osborne to the nation, keeping only as a permanent memorial to his mother those apartments in which she had lived and died. The State rooms on the ground floor and the immense Indian Durbar room were to be opened to the public on certain visiting days. The stables and adjoining paddocks were to be converted into a Naval College for Cadets, and the large wing of the house adapted as a convalescent home for officers of the army and navy invalided home from foreign service.

Princess Beatrice could of course continue to live in her own wing and Princess Louise (the Duchess of Argyll) also had a house on the estate which had been given to her by her mother. Both these sisters, no longer young, were extremely angry with the King for disregarding the Queen's wishes. They argued that the King's action had entirely destroyed the privacy they had hitherto enjoyed and had in fact converted their quiet homes into quite undesirable residences. But the King had made up his mind and beyond offering to extend the grounds around Princess Beatrice's residence he was not prepared to do anything more.[6]

His first public function was performed three weeks after the Queen's death when he drove in the full panoply of State for the opening of the new session of Parliament on 14th February 1901. This was a function which the Queen had often neglected after the death of Prince Albert. Despite angry scenes with Gladstone, who minced no words as Prime Minister and described it as a dereliction by the Queen of her public duty, Her Majesty completely ignored his rebukes: no more than half a dozen times in the course of her forty widowed years had she bothered to take part in this important ceremonial. To the King it was not merely a time-honoured custom but a clear and essential indication to the people of the Sovereign's central role in the constitution. He was resolved that it should be maintained, and he insisted on reading personally the Speech from the Throne.

Although tradition had for him always been sacrosanct, in one instance, at the very beginning of his reign, he strove to depart from it. This was over the Declaration pronounced in Parliament by each Sovereign. The wording of the Declaration had been set out in the Bill of Rights in 1689 after the flight of the Roman Catholic King James the Second, and its purpose was to ensure the succession of his Protestant daughter Mary the Second and her husband William the Third.

King Edward regarded the words as offensive. They offered, he said, a gratuitous insult to his Roman Catholic subjects. It was obnoxious in his view to assert publicly that 'the invocation or adoration of the Virgin Mary or any other saint and the sacrifice of the Mass as they are now used in the Church of Rome are superstitious and idolatrous', and to vow that his Declaration was made 'without any evasion, equivocation or mental reservation whatever, and without any dispensation past or future or possibility of it from the Pope or any other authority.'

He was told that no alteration could be made except by a fresh Act of Parliament and there was not time for this to be done before the opening of his first Parliament. So with the utmost distaste the King had no alternative but to read the objectionable words. He lowered his voice as he did so and resolved that no successor of his should suffer a similar embarrassment and humiliation. He discussed this on the very next day with the aged and ailing Prime Minister, Lord Salisbury, who nodded his white beard placatorily and told the King that the Cabinet recognised the desirability of making 'some change'. But the lukewarmness of Salisbury's words did not escape the King: the Cabinet's view seemed by no means as pronounced as his own. He was insistent that a revision must be made, and as a result of his persistence in the summer of that year a committee of nine peers was set up to decide on a new form of Declaration. When the King read their report in the newspapers he was extremely angry. He wrote at once to the Lord Chancellor, Lord Halsbury, to ask why it was published without any previous indication to him of this 'important matter concerning the Sovereign regarding which he ought to have been consulted'.

He was moreover far from satisfied with the revision. Some modification had been made in the old wording, but in the main it still retained much that was bound to be offensive to the Roman Catholics. Salisbury was told bluntly that the Declaration should be made shorter and should be confined merely to the King's determination to uphold the Protestant faith. He insisted further 'that the Government should come to no decision respecting the precise words without his being previously consulted', and was sternly critical of 'the Lord Chancellor's bungling from the beginning'.

Now it was Salisbury who was not prepared to agree. Despite the King's repeated efforts in the succeeding years, it was not until three months after his death in 1910 that an Act was at last passed through both Houses of Parliament to replace the old Declaration by the following words: 'I do solemnly and sincerely in the presence of God profess, testify, and declare that I am a faithful Protestant, and that I will, according to the true intent of the enactments to secure the Protestant succession to the Throne of My Realm, uphold and maintain such enactments to the best of my power.'

It was what King Edward had wanted.

CHAPTER 3

The Country at War

The Edwardian Age, which one associates with gaiety and frivolity and unlicensed extravagance, began astonishingly during a war and ended nine years later within sight of yet another war—a war that involved the entire world and was regarded as the greatest war in history until the one that came a generation later.

The South African war had been in progress for a year and a quarter when Edward came to the throne and it still dragged on—this little war against a handful of Boers which no one had regarded as more than a punitive operation. It had in fact not yet run half its course and was to go on for still another year and a half.

The worst phase, however, was over. In the opening months the Boers, with surprising speed, had besieged Ladysmith, Mafeking and Kimberley. In Kitchener's view the officers of the British army seemed to regard the war too much like a game of polo 'with intervals for afternoon tea'. But by the accession all that had changed. The beleaguered towns had been relieved, Johannesburg had been captured and Kruger had fled—yet the war dragged on. Kitchener's forecast a year before, in the summer of 1900, that it would end 'in another fortnight or three weeks' had been hopelessly wrong. Why, the King demanded now, had not the British armies, numbering close on half a million men, been able to dispose of the

Boer forces, which at no time numbered more than 65,000?

It was causing the acutest embarrassment and distress both to King and country. As each fresh contingent in khaki marched through the streets on their way to a port of embarkation, the crowd cheered, shouted their goodbyes and prayed that it would soon all be over. After the procession had passed one saw only long, dejected faces. Voices were raised in angry complaint in the clubs and country houses. In almost every country in Europe, Britain's reputation had suffered seriously. Popular sympathy was entirely with the Boers. The Tsar, in a letter to the King in June 1901, addressing him as 'My dearest Uncle Bertie,' wrote: 'You remember, of course, at the time when War broke out what a strong feeling of animosity against England arose throughout the world,' and now, after two years of fighting, he went on, 'a small people are desperately defending their country, a part of their land is devastated, their families flocked together in camps, their farms burnt. . . . How many thousands of gallant young Englishmen have already perished out there!'

The King answered sharply: 'Supposing that Sweden, after spending years in the accumulation of enormous armaments and magazines, had suddenly forbidden you to move a single regiment in Finland,* and on your refusing to obey had invaded Russia in *three* places, would you have abstained from defending yourself, and when war had once begun by that Swedish invasion, would you not have felt bound, both in prudence and honour, to continue military operations until the enemy had submitted?'[5] What assurance was there, he asked, that the Boers would not do the same thing again as soon as they had accumulated fresh armaments, unless the war was fought to a finish now?

In Germany too there was the warmest enthusiasm for the Boers and widespread discontent at the German Government's attitude of passive neutrality. At meeting after meeting all over that country resolutions were passed calling for military intervention in support of the Boers. The Kaiser, another of King Edward's nephews, had already sent a

* Finland was at that time under Russian rule.

congratulatory telegram to Kruger after the Jameson raid which preceded the war, offering to send German troops to protect the Transvaal. It brought him a sharp rebuke from his grandmother, Queen Victoria. The German Press was full of accounts of British atrocities against Boer women and children, and Joseph Chamberlain, the British Colonial Secretary, greatly inflamed the atmosphere by countering with sweeping accusations not only against Germany but against almost every country in Europe. This widespread hostility was outrageously one-sided. Boer commandos on horseback had ranged the countryside in groups, pillaging convoys and razing camps. They attacked and disappeared. The British dead were stripped of their uniforms which were then worn by the Boers for devious deceptions.

In a belated endeavour to pour oil upon these troubled waters, the Kaiser asked King Edward to send the Prince of Wales (later King George the Fifth) on an official visit to Berlin. The Prince arrived on 26th January 1902 and was warmly received. The German Foreign Minister, Baron von Richthofen, begged his countrymen not to forget their kinship with the English and quoted a German army officer's tribute to the British for their great humanity to their Boer prisoners in a camp in Ceylon.[23] This was endorsed by the German General Count Waldersee while on a visit to England, when he referred to the considerate and kindly attitude of the British troops to the Boer population. King Edward was nevertheless greatly irritated by the continuous criticisms in Germany and bluntly told Baron von Eckardstein, the German Chargé d'Affaires in London, that he could no longer give much weight to the long letters he received from the Kaiser assuring him of his friendship for England, and there could be no more question of Germany and England co-operating in any conceivable matter.[24]

The hostility of Holland was of course understandable, but even France joined in the chorus of attacks—indeed scarcely a single neutral country on the Continent had a word to say in support of Britain.

In Britain itself there were angry denunciations of the

war by a vocal pro-Boer section, of whom the principal spokesman was Lloyd George. The Liberal Party as a whole did not go quite as far. Sir Henry Campbell-Bannerman, its Leader, spoke of the 'methods of barbarism' in South Africa, condemned the insistence on unconditional surrender, and strongly supported peace by negotiation. The King, well aware that the feeling of depression was caused by the dragging inconclusiveness of the war, since the end was not in sight even now, wrote to Lord Salisbury: 'The strain on the resources of the country is becoming very great. Additional taxation must ensue, and the amount of troops now in South Africa is becoming most serious, should they at any emergency be required elsewhere.'

He went into the details of the operations most critically. He referred to the dissatisfaction felt over the horses that had been sent out. To the Secretary of State for War (Mr Brodrick) he wrote: 'The "show up" about the horses purchased for South Africa is a great scandal and even worse than I thought after reading Friday's debate in the House of Commons. How can a man like Captain Hartigan, who passed the Remounts, be still employed? Justly the War Office are seriously to blame, and there has been an official blindness as to what was going on in the War Office which is very reprehensible.' Four days later he wrote again: 'There is no doubt that someone will have to be hung for it.' It is evident from these rebukes how much of his mother's angry watchfulness he had inherited.

Peace finally came on 31st May 1902. The Boer republics of Transvaal and Orange River Colony were incorporated in the British Empire, but the terms otherwise were generous. All farms damaged during the war were to be restored and a grant of £3,000,000 was made for the resettlement of Boers in their homes. Representative government was to be set up as soon as possible in the Boer provinces. The friction between the two races was thus ended.

The King's joy was as intense as that of the people. He turned his thoughts now to his Coronation, the date of which he had fixed for 26th June 1902.

CHAPTER 4

Horse-buses and Flower Girls

Surprisingly enough the long, and often infuriating, months of war did not affect the life of the people in a cataclysmic way. For one thing it was remote. The resources of the nation in manpower and material were drawn on without causing grave shortages. Business went on very much as usual. The rich continued to get richer and the round of entertaining in the country houses as well as the season in London suffered neither interruption nor diminution. True there was hardly a family in this section of the community without at least one member serving with the forces as either officers (all of them moustached) or nurses, and extracts from their letters were read out to friends amid murmurs of sympathy or disgust.

In London one saw bicycles, some of them ridden by women, threading their way perilously amid the horse-drawn four-wheelers and buses. Hansoms kept overturning, especially along St James's Street, which was steep, very slippery when it rained, and rarely sanded. The horses shied and bolted whenever they encountered the noisy, terrifying but fortunately all too rare motor-car. One saw Claude Hay, the brother of Lord Kinnoul, driving through Dover Street in a large motor, or Lord Carnarvon or Charles Rolls in a 50-horsepower Napier, crawling, spluttering and constantly breaking down. The King had a car specially built for him by Daimler a year or two before and occasionally drove to Windsor for the week-end; when he set out on the longer journey to Sandringham, he had tyre trouble at Finchley and the car had to be hauled along to a near-by bicycle shop for the tyre's repair. The hansom drivers were scornful: 'They are just playthings,' they sneered. 'They'll never beat the old horse.' Nor was one safe from the bicycle which, after gliding through the interstices of the congested traffic, had a way of making its presence known by colliding with the backs of pedestrians, then picking its way timidly across streets unmarked by beacons and zebra crossings. In Piccadilly the pet goat of the Rothschilds ambled every afternoon along the roadway, dodging the horse-buses as best it could, unconcerned because the drivers were careful not to harm it for fear of losing the brace of pheasants that Leopold Rothschild presented to every driver and conductor on New Year's Day. The small, narrow buses of assorted colours, each line bearing its own distinctive hue, had a reserved box-seat for their regular customers beside the driver who complained constantly that all their best horses had been commandeered for the cavalry and sent off to South Africa. It was not an easy time for the pedestrian. Horses hooves spattered them with mud; clubmen derived a certain amount of fun by walking near the kerb in Regent Street for a bet, the money going to the man with the fewest splashes. During a walk from Verrey's, near Oxford Circus, to Piccadilly Circus, R. D. Blumenfeld records that one of the clubmen, a Belgian diplomat, finished up with five blobs of mud on his high choker collar and three on his face.[53] In the quieter residential sections of the West End and beyond, one found straw laid on the road to deaden the noise of the traffic if someone was lying ill in the adjoining house or a woman was expecting a baby.

At the Eros fountain in Piccadilly Circus a score of flower girls, blowzy, pink-cheeked, in shawls and bonnets amid their wondrous display of flowers, hailed monocled, top-hatted men to buy a gardenia for their button-holes. Almost all the men were in long frock-coats with short lapels, reaching up to their high collars and stocks, fancy waist-coats, striped trousers, and of course spats over their boots. They were not the only ones in top-hats: everybody seemed to wear them, bank clerks, shop-walkers, cab-drivers. And, because of the King, most men wore beards, neatly trimmed like his. In the streets around this hub the theatres, more abundant then, stood almost shoulder to shoulder, and noisily buskers entertained the queues with banjos and songs and somersaults.

The King was fond of the theatre. Only rarely did a serious play draw him. He went to see *Arms and the Man* by Bernard Shaw and thought him 'a damned crank'. Shaw enjoyed little success then—hardly any of his plays ran for even fifty nights. Much more to the King's taste were musical comedies: he found the lilting melodies haunting, the girls of the chorus, so decidedly feminine then, quite captivating. Young men in the Guards and elderly members of such clubs as White's and Boodle's went night after night to the same seat in the stalls merely to gaze through their opera glasses at one of the girls. After the performance they trooped to the stage-door with bouquets of flowers and large boxes of chocolates and handed them to the stage-door keeper with their card and a sovereign for his pains. Patiently the young men waited, possibly in the snow or a heavy shower of rain, wearing white ties and tails—everybody dressed then for the stalls and the circle. 'Stage-door Johnnies' they were called, some called them 'mashers' or 'lady-killers'. Behind and around them stood a huddle of waiting hansoms, the horses pawing the ground and neighing, their bells jingling, the dim street lighting falling lightly on the brass of their harness. No policemen, no traffic wardens moved them on. Suddenly, in the shabby back-door of the theatre, one of the girls would appear, feathered and cloaked and radiant; and one of the men, white-haired perhaps or blushingly youthful, would step forward, his cloak flowing, his arm extended to take hers: his moment had come.

Most of the theatres had music to offer and there was

always the music hall, sprinkled so liberally about the West End and within easy reach at Islington, Kennington and Fulham, and of course the Met. in Edgware Road. Dan Leno was doing a skit on Sherlock Holmes at Drury Lane, while William Gillet handled the role seriously at the Lyceum; there was Gus Elen, Marie Lloyd, and Bransby Williams, even in 1902, was presenting Dickens characters and was to continue to do so for sixty more years. In Leicester Square stood the Alhambra and the Empire, the resort of the *jeunesse dorée* and the *demi-mondaines* in their large ostrich-feathered hats and fluffy boas. Its wide Promenade behind the stalls was thronged and noisy. All the young bloods were there and when they got obstreperous, as they often did, the burly chuckers-out came and threw them out. One young blood dealt with thus brusquely was Winston Churchill, destined to be one of Britain's greatest Prime Ministers. This was the mecca of every masculine hope as the men languished in jungle hut or *dâk* bungalow, bronzed and possibly wizened in the far-flung outposts of an Empire that has since been merged into a Commonwealth, and this was where they spent their first evening of home leave. For years the dream had sustained them and the fulfilment far surpassed their expectations, as, ageing now and in creased evening suits that no longer fitted them, they came for their longed-for fling. But to their wives and sisters and mothers the Promenade was a cesspool of iniquity. Brazen, painted hussies, so they were told, slunk slowly by, their eyes questing, their glances beckoning, their silken dresses brushing gently against every man they passed. Relentlessly the wives of Britain's proconsuls, supported by the clergy of various denominations, strove to get the Promenade closed, but the resistance was too strong. The Empire was a national institution and it continued to flourish throughout the Edwardian age. To many it was a club: they dropped in for half an hour, expecting to run into old friends who had last written from Calcutta or Quetta or Kuala Lumpur, glancing only occasionally at the stage to learn from Vesta Tilley, the male impersonator turned out by Savile Row, what the best dressed man should be wearing and to come away humming such haunting refrains as 'I'm Burlington Bertie, I rise at ten-thirty, and saunter along like a toff'.

Within a pace of Leicester Square was Daly's, also purveying musical comedy (with Lily Elsie in *The Merry Widow* in 1907) and the Hippodrome, at that time a music hall. Round the corner, along the Strand, were the Tivoli, the Adelphi, the Vaudeville, and then the Gaiety, which stood, in a domed magnificence all its own, opposite the Lyceum. It was rebuilt in 1903 and King Edward and Queen Alexandra roused the audience to the wildest excitement by coming to the opening. This had been his favourite theatre when he was Prince of Wales. Here he had seen the light, lilting musical diversions of George Edwardes—*The Orchid, Our Miss Gibbs*, and relays of very lovely Gaiety Girls. These were the girls who made the best marriages. Among those who came to the stage-door with flowers and boxes of chocolates were many young peers and heirs of peers. Eagerly they took one, then another, of the girls out to supper, for suppers played a vital part in London's night life then. There were whispers and laughter. Cupid was in attendance. Denise Orme (real name Jessie Smithers) became the Baroness Churston; Sylvia Storey became the Countess Poulett; Olive May (real name Meatyard) married Lord Victor Paget, heir presumptive to the Marquess of Anglesey; and there were others. Some married millionaires, like Hilda Harris who married Drummond of Drummond's Bank, others married men who later became millionaires. Gaby Delys, the dancer, was the mistress of King Manoel, the last King of Portugal.

The courtship was always begun across the supper table. Theatreland was strewn with elegant and luxurious restaurants to which one could go after the theatre. The French dishes were delightfully tasty, the wine excellent. King Edward favoured Rule's, a select, secluded place in Maiden Lane behind the Strand. Victorianism lingered here amid the draperies and the abundance of small, often tiny, pictures on the walls. It was in the main the haunt of

Bohemians and he came not with the Queen, but usually with a party of friends, or one of the many ladies whose company delighted him. There was only one private room here, but at Kettner's and the Café Royal, at Solferino's as at so many of the other restaurants in the West End, there were at least half a dozen private rooms where one could take an actress for an undisturbed *tête-à-tête*. These rooms were small as a rule. There was, beside the table at which they supped, just a narrow, uncomfortable settee: it must have been extremely restricting for these stout people (and the girls too were generally stout) to recline on after the waiter had said good-night and wheeled out the ice pail, the empty bottles and the soiled plates. The women were heavily corseted and whale-boned, the formidable contraption stretching from under the arms down to the upper reaches of the thighs; to lace it effectively into the required hour-glass shape demanded the combined efforts of two personal maids while a third spent many hours evolving the elaborate hair style then fashionable. No woman could be expected to emerge with her hair ruffled when the evening ended. Similarly today a girl arriving with the current wind-blown hair-do could hardly emerge from a private supper room with her hair elegantly combed and brushed. It is puzzling therefore how the Edwardian women managed to engage in a clandestine romance. In the more expensive restaurants things were more considerately planned. The private rooms were large enough to seat a dozen at table, but if there happened to be only two, then after supper had been cleared, a maid, supplied by the restaurant, would slip into the room, touch a button on the panelling and bring down an ample bed. Behind a screen the maid would attend to the lady's disrobing and help her again afterwards into her dress. These private rooms were also available for tea. Where else were the couples to go? There were very few flats; when more were available it was possible for a man of means to rent one for his exclusive use; and the motor-car in time enabled him to take his lady-love to a near-by country hotel. In the eighteenth and earlier centuries most of the London taverns around Covent Garden provided private rooms for aristocrats and their lady friends. King Edward's predecessor, Charles the Second, frequently made use of them.

At Kettner's a large private room upstairs is known even now as the King Edward Room. He used it mostly, they say, to entertain a party of friends, numbering often as many as ten; they also say that there used to be a secret passage into Kettner's from the Palace Theatre, which is almost opposite.

These private rooms survived the coming of motors and the buildings of flats; they even survived the First World War. Small Soho restaurants were honeycombed with them throughout the twenties.

Kettner used to be Napoleon III's chef in Paris. He came to London a year or so before Napoleon fell. During his exile in Chislehurst the ex-Emperor often entertained his friends here, bringing as his guests Disraeli, Bulwer Lytton, Lord Derby—and no doubt he introduced King Edward to the delights and secrets of the establishment.

Oscar Phillipe presided at the Cavour in Leicester Square. He was illiterate, but that did not affect the admirable quality of his food. In a little garden at the back of the restaurant where a news cinema now stands he grew his own parsley and tarragon, chives and sorrel: in terms of land values it must have been quite the most expensive kitchen-garden in the world. His restaurant was filled with *demi-mondaines* 'of the highest grade', always well dressed, less strident in their make-up, less brazen in their approach. Romano was at the restaurant that bore his name in the Strand; there was the Globe in Coventry Street, another haunt of the *demi-mondaines*; the Café de la Régence, also in Coventry street; and near it the Hotel Mathis (where Lyons Corner House is now); the Café de l'Etoile in Great Windmill Street; the Provence and the Europe in Leicester Square; Pinoli's in Wardour Street; Hatchett's in Piccadilly; the Monico in Piccadilly Circus; and of course the Criterion, where the supper hour brought a gay bustling throng to the American bar for its special delicacy, grilled pigs' feet.

Each of these places had its own group of regulars. To their usual tables they brought their friends because the food was good, the cellars filled with choice vintages, and the prices far from exorbitant. For as little as £2 a young man-about-town could sit down with a pretty little chorus girl to a seven course supper, consisting of *hors d'œuvres*, soup, trout *meunière*, lamb cutlets with peas and potatoes, then partridge *en casserole* with salad, followed by artichokes *hollandais*, and finally ice *en corbeille* with *petits fours*; champagne enlivened the meal and liqueurs were supplied with their coffee—all of it for just £2.[69] There was no problem about finding a hansom to see the girl home, though it was always possible that the cabman would be drunk.

If one wanted a more lavish meal, at the Carlton for instance, M. Echenard would prepare a special menu for the young man and his girl and he could have a quiet *tête-à-tête* in a corner, with a Russian Grand Duke (there were so many Russian Grand Dukes) at the next table, French and Austrian counts and German Princes bowing and smiling to each other as they came in. The meal would cost more, but not much more: a seven-course dinner, beginning with oysters and followed by soup, *filet de sole* (served in piecrust with vermicelli and crayfish tails, flavoured with champagne and parmesan), *noisettes de chevreuil Diane* (a delicious sauce), *suprême de volaille au paprika*, then ortolans cooked in an earthenware *cocotte* and served with grapes as a foundation, *friandises*, and *Bénédictines rosés* (cherries in a pink casing), champagne to drink—all of it costing sixpence under £3 for two, with the coffee included in that sum, but served while one reclined in large armchairs in the cream and pink lounge where a pale blue light fell on the palms and the band played a Hungarian march or a *mazurka*.

CHAPTER 5

Modernising the Palaces

The King gave his early attention to the redecoration and renovation of the Royal Palaces.

Buckingham Palace, rarely used by Queen Victoria through her long widowhood, had become unspeakably shabby. The rooms were so dark and dismal that the King called it 'The Sepulchre'. The imitation marble walls of the entrance hall were discoloured with age. The State rooms had not been cleaned for years. It was in one of the guest rooms here that the Shah of Persia, during his State visit in 1873, had sacrificed a sheep to the intense annoyance of Queen Victoria. The King ordered that these rooms should now be fumigated.

The suite once occupied by Prince Albert, and left untouched since his death forty years before, was now dismantled. The King intended to occupy these rooms himself. His father's clothes, dressing-gowns, shoes, hair brushes, and other relics were removed to the Round Tower at Windsor Castle or to the rooms preserved at Osborne as a memorial to his parents. Most of the Queen's personal possessions she had herself taken to Osborne. The rest, chiefly bronze statuettes, paper-weights and articles of small intrinsic value, were distributed among members of the Royal family. Queen Alexandra preferred to play no part whatsoever in these alterations, but left the changes entirely to the King. In all, the redecoration took more than a year to complete, and it was not until April 1902 that His Majesty and Queen Alexandra were able to vacate Marlborough House, where they had lived for forty years since their marriage, and move into Buckingham Palace.

At Windsor Castle too very considerable cleaning as well as redecoration had to be done. The sanitation, heating, lighting and general standard of comfort were hopelessly antiquated. Here too there was a vast quantity of Queen Victoria's keepsakes. She had reverently preserved every reminder of her childhood and of her married life. These accumulations represented more than seventy years of sentimental memories. There were dolls, bric-à-brac, endless photographs and miniatures, china, dresses, slippers, parasols, feathers: every wardrobe, every drawer, every table and mantelpiece in the rooms she used were full of the treasured tokens she had been reluctant to discard. The King decided to dispose of them. Here too he took over his father's suite, in which every evening since his death Prince Albert's clothes had been set out for him to wear, and his medicine bottle and a spoon placed in readiness for his use.

At Balmoral all the tartan was removed from the drawing-room and the statue of John Brown, the dour Scots gillie, whose relationship with Queen Victoria had caused the most embarrassing gossip—King Edward wanted no reminder of him.

The redecoration at these three residences, as also of Holyrood Palace in Edinburgh, the King supervised personally. He brought into use many valuable but neglected pieces of furniture belonging to the royal collection and selected some magnificent paintings from the considerable range of pictures acquired by Charles I and others. For the first time for nearly a century the palaces became worthy settings for their display. 'In arranging these pictures,' Sir Lionel Cust records,[17] 'I found it useless to ask the King if I should hang this *there* or another *here*, and so on. His mind could not take it in. "Offer it up," he would say, and "offered up" he would come to see and perhaps put his head on one side, all with a twinkle in his eye, and say, "That is not *amiss*", or perhaps he would at once say that he did not like it. He enjoyed sitting in a room with the men working about him, and liked giving directions himself as to the actual position of pictures.'

There were a great many protests, not only from members of the Royal family but from friends of Queen Victoria, over the sweeping changes made by the King; even the Press was critical, but when the work was completed there was, Cust states, unstinting praise at the transformation to elegance and dignity of what were once just mournful mausoleums.

The King took a special pride in taking his guests round to look at the pictures and to admire the cabinets of miniatures, the settees and commodes. His knowledge of art was slight—he readily admitted this—but he had a great love for beautiful things as well as beautiful women. To the inherited family portraits, Queen Victoria had added innumerable photographs and paintings of obscure Guelph relatives—all these were retained by the King. With his astonishing memory he was able to identify even the remotest members of the smallest Saxon duchies.

The occasional, extremely formal afternoon 'Drawing Rooms' of Queen Victoria, solemn, dull, frigid and oppressive, the King felt were quite unsuitable for these new brighter and gayer settings. He substituted levées and evening receptions that were dazzling in splendour. Queen Victoria had allowed no talking: only when she spoke was a guest permitted to reply; at her larger gatherings muted whispers went on at the far end of the room in the uneasy hope that they would not be overheard by her. The rooms reverberated now with merriment and laughter. Even on the most formal State occasions the King moved among his guests with a cheerful word and an exchanged jest. Lord Esher thought that perhaps the King was a little 'too human'.

Among the King's friends there were many whose very presence at Court caused eyebrows to be raised in astonishment. A number of these were Jews—three of them, the Sassoon brothers, were rich merchant traders with business interests in the East; another was Ernest Cassel, a German Jew whose father was a banker in Cologne. Cassel was considered to be the King's closest friend. He came to England at the early age of eighteen, worked with a financial firm in the City and set up his own business in 1884 when he was only thirty-two. His financial genius was undisputed, his activities far-reaching. He organised the finances of Uruguay, was responsible for three Mexican loans, financed the Vickers absorption of the Maxim-Nordenfelt Company and arranged for the construction of the Central London Underground railway. Shrewd, blunt and reserved, he was disliked by those who knew little of his munificent gifts to charity. He helped to found the King Edward VII sanatorium for consumptives at Midhurst in Sussex, set up the Radium Institute, and established an Educational Trust for the education of workers. In all he gave away more than £2,000,000 during his lifetime.

He had become a naturalised British subject some years before the King's accession and in 1902, as a mark of his esteem for Cassel, His Majesty created him a Privy Councillor. After the King's death this was challenged as Cassel was British neither by birth nor by parentage and it was argued that he was debarred by the Act of Settlement of 1701 from being a Privy Councillor. After much argument it was decided eventually that the disqualification had been repealed by subsequent legislation. King Edward further conferred on him the Grand Cross of the Order of St Michael and St George in 1902, of the Victorian Order in 1906 and of the Bath in 1909. His services to the King were considerable. His Majesty benefited greatly from his sound financial advice; Cassel in fact practically controlled all His Majesty's investments.

The King attended the wedding of Cassel's only child, his daughter Maud, to Wilfrid Ashley, M.P., later Lord Mount Temple; and was godfather to their elder daughter Edwina (as her name indicates): she became a member of the royal family by her marriage to Lord Louis Mount-batten, later Earl Mountbatten of Burma.

Among these friends there were some of quite humble birth and the criticism often made was that not all of them were reputable. It should not be overlooked, however, that also in the circle were many members of the old English aristocracy, such as the eighth Duke of Devonshire, great uncle of Lady Dorothy Macmillan; Lord Esher; Lord Carrington; Lord de Grey (later the Marquess of Ripon); the Hon. Evan Charteris; the Hon. Harry Stonor; Lord Marcus Beresford; and Lord Redesdale, the grandfather of the six Mitford girls who included Nancy (the writer), Unity (a friend of Hitler), Jessica (who was married to Esmond Romilly, the Communist nephew of Winston Churchill), and Deborah (who married the eleventh Duke of Devonshire).

With their names in Burke and Debrett they would appear to be acceptable enough, but they were not to Queen Victoria. She regarded most of them as being too high-spirited, wild and irresponsible: the Marquess of Waterford, for example, a young Irish peer, startled society by eloping with the wife of his best friend; his brother Lord Charles Beresford was impetuous and quick-tempered—his friend-ship with King Edward had been close for a great many years, they went to India together, but later there was a most violent quarrel between them over the Countess of Warwick (then Lady Brooke), who at the end of a long and intimate relationship with the King (when he was Prince of Wales) found a successor in Lord Charles Beresford. Divorce was averted by a reconciliation between Beresford, and his wife, but a letter to him of bitter reproach from Lady Brooke fell into the hands of Lady Charles Beresford who promptly consulted her solicitor. The Prince, appealed to by Lady Brooke in her anguish, strove to prevent a scan-dal, but Beresford stood angrily by his wife: he resented her exclusion from the Prince's set and, after calling the Prince a coward and a blackguard in an embarrassing interview, raised his fist to strike him.[44] The Prime Minister, Lord

Salisbury, was dragged in. Queen Victoria had to be informed and the Prince wrote to Waterford: 'I can never forgive the conduct of your brother and his wife.' Scandal was luckily avoided.

Another friend was Lord Hartington, the Duke of Devonshire's heir, who managed to keep several mistresses going at the same time. Still another was Colonel Valentine Baker, brother of Sir Samuel Baker the explorer. The colonel, older than the Prince by some years, was a distinguished, hard-riding cavalry officer in the 10th Hussars, and had fought in the Crimean war. The highest honours in the Army seemed within his reach when on a stupid impulse he made an indecent assault on a pretty girl while travelling in a railway carriage from Midhurst to London. The girl screamed—there were no communication cords in those days (1875); after a struggle she got out of the carriage and, clinging to the door with her feet on the flatboard, kept on screaming until the train reached the next station. Baker was found guilty, sent to prison for a year and dismissed from the Army. Queen Victoria had thus yet further proof to justify her criticism of her son's friends. But Edward remained loyal to Valentine Baker: that was his outstanding trait, no matter what happened he stood by his friends in their misfortunes. He tried to get Baker the command of the British Army in Egypt after the conquest of that country in 1882, but the War Office refused to countenance it. An odd twist in the story is that Lord Kitchener as a young lieutenant met Baker's daughter Mary when she was a child of ten; by the time she was sixteen she was deeply in love with Kitchener and, it is said, he was with her; but she died less than two years later: Kitchener never married and wore a miniature portrait of the girl for many years.[51]

The King was quite indifferent to the criticism levelled against his choice of friends. Despite his love of ceremonial on State occasions, in his private life he liked to have around him men and women who were gay and amusing, with a charm of manner, a flash of wit, a keen intelligence and a grasp of affairs—the range covered a wide field from sport to finance. After all his mother, despite her prim dignity, had always been indifferent to the comments made about John Brown, who occupied such a privileged place in her life after the death of Prince Albert: he was familiar in his manner, insisted on being treated with deference and respect, but in his turn was off-hand and rude to almost everybody. This merely amused Queen Victoria, who often quoted the things he said, making use even of his slang vocabulary. She took him everywhere with her, even on her annual trips to the Riviera, and gave away miniatures of John Brown set in diamonds as a special mark of her favour. The scurrilous man called her 'Mrs John Brown'.

Not quite of the King's circle was Lord Rosebery, who had been Liberal Prime Minister a few years before Edward came to the throne. Their association had been close enough once: when they were both much younger, Knollys, the King's Private Secretary, wrote to Rosebery to ask if he would make his London house available for the Prince of Wales and his brother the Duke of Edinburgh to entertain their actress friends there. Rosebery replied curtly that the house was too small and said he hoped the matter would not be raised again.[18] Rosebery, by no means a prude, liked and admired the Prince but did not care for his brother. Once, at a party in Mayfair at the house of Frank Lawley of the *Daily Telegraph* at which the Prince and his brother were also guests together with some actress friends, Rosebery found that the drinking, cock-fighting and other amusements were to go on all through the night and left early. He preferred to be on the fringe of this set, but he was kept informed by Knollys of the Prince's many escapades. Nevertheless he was close enough for the Prince of Wales to act as godfather at the christening of Rosebery's heir, who was in consequence named Albert Edward.

Nor should the Marquis de Soveral, the Portuguese Minister in London, be overlooked. Tall, dark, blue-chinned (and so nicknamed 'The Blue Monkey'), fiercely moustached and always with a white button-hole, he was a great favourite of the King's because of his gaiety and his ready wit. Once, when his name had been omitted inadvertently from the Sandringham guest list, the King telegraphed for him and asked Soveral on his arrival: 'Why did you have to wait for an invitation?' The ready reply was: 'Well, Sir, I had got as far as my door when your command arrived.'

Another constantly in the King's company was the Italian marine artist, Commendatore Eduardo de Martino, who had been Painter-in-Ordinary to Queen Victoria. His role was to act as a Court Jester to the King and to serve as a butt for His Majesty's jibes. He seemed to enjoy it and roused a lot of laughter with his very bad English.

There were a great many lovely women in the King's life. He enjoyed being with them. It was often thought, and said, that he greatly preferred spending his time with women rather than with men. For one who participated so eagerly in such essentially manly sports as shooting, deer-stalking, pig-sticking (during his Indian trip for example), yachting and attending race meetings, the generalisation is a little too facile. There was of course a noticeable difference in his attitude to the sexes; men came into the category of friends, women he regarded chiefly as playthings: they provided a lighter and often a romantic diversion. The attitude may be likened to that of an Oriental Sultan—there was indeed much of that in him; but he was more enlightened, being of the West, yet not enlightened enough to accept women as man's full equal. To the end of his life he remained hostile to their adopting male activities: it robbed them of their femininity and their appeal, he said. Though progressive in his acceptance of the many changes wrought in the life around him by the remarkable inventions of the time, all of which he adopted with eagerness and alacrity, in this one respect he totally rejected any change that would cause women to surrender the role of enchantress, which he felt nature had assigned to them.

It should be remembered that his upbringing was narrow and stifling. So-called governors, who were in fact stern disciplinarians drawn from the top ranks of the Army, had been expressly instructed to deny him, throughout his boyhood and adolescence, the companionship of others of his own age. Only thus, it was felt, could he be insulated from contamination. He was debarred from participating in games. The curriculum of education, drawn up by Prince Albert himself, was designed to fill every hour of the day with mental occupation and improvement. Science, applied mechanics, law, history and three European languages were imposed as an essential supplement to what a boy was normally required to learn. The strain of this harsh and cruel upbringing proved oppressive. The child found it impossible to absorb and retain all that was pumped into his immature brain and from time to time, unable to endure it any longer, the young Prince rebelled and was subjected to still further disciplining. There were inevitably recurrent nervous outbursts.

It is easy to imagine his resentment and acute unhappiness. Even on his seventeenth birthday, when he was gazetted an Honorary Colonel and made a Knight of the Garter, he was handed a memorandum, signed by both the Queen and his father, which greatly increased the restraints. 'You are placed,' it stated, 'under the supervision and guidance of a Governor selected from among the members of the aristocracy and the superior officers of the army . . . The equerries will take and receive their orders from the Governor. You will never leave the house without reporting yourself, and he will settle who is to accompany you, and will give general directions as to the disposition of the day.'[3]

In the two and a half years that followed he was sent to no less than three universities—Edinburgh, Oxford and Cambridge—at each of which he stayed for only a term or two. At none of these was he allowed either to mix with the other undergraduates or to participate in any way in the social life of the university. Any attempt to break away from this strict routine was instantly reported. His father was informed that the Prince had become interested in playing billiards and cards, in smoking cigars and in 'the foolish vanity of dandyism'.

In the summer of 1861, during the vacation at Cambridge, he was sent on an infantry training course with the Guards at the Curragh, near Dublin. Some of the other young officers at the camp managed to smuggle a pretty young actress named Nellie Clifden into the Prince's rooms. The Prince resisted the temptation for a time, but his sudden release from constraint, the exhilarating discovery that he was free of tutors and governors and was able to indulge himself, unwatched and unchided, made him succumb. A liaison developed. The gossip in time reached the ears of his father. Not knowing what to believe, Prince Albert decided to go and see his son, who by now had returned to Cambridge. For some days Prince Albert had been suffering from a very heavy catarrh, pains in his limbs and a continuous headache. He nevertheless rose from his sickbed and undertook the long, exhausting journey to Cambridge. His son confessed at once.[44] He adored both his father and mother (surprisingly enough seeing that he got neither sympathy nor understanding from them) and on no account was he prepared to lie. The ordeal was too much for Prince Albert. His condition became worse and shortly after his return home he collapsed and died. He was only forty-two. Queen Victoria never forgave her son for this. To the end of her life she firmly clung to the belief that Bertie had contributed to if not actually caused her beloved Albert's death. She did not get in touch with her son while Prince Albert lay dying: it was her daughter Alice who sent for him without the Queen's knowledge, and afterwards Queen Victoria's only wish was to keep the boy out of her sight. She talked to the Prime Minister, Lord Palmerston, about sending him away and it was arranged that Edward should travel.

The Prince set out for the Near East within a few weeks of his father's death. She insisted that he must observe the 'very strictest *incognito*'. He was sent in the care of his stern guardian, General Bruce, and was away for five months.

How far was the boy damaged by this rigorous upbringing and to what extent did it affect his outlook and his behaviour? He certainly never became either the good or the learned man his father, and of course also his mother, wanted him to be. He fell far short of the paragon they envisaged and had tried so hard to create. Though the plan was well-intentioned, it was one of Prince Albert's gravest errors and the wonder is that his son Edward was able in time to recover from it and shoulder his duties seriously and conscientiously. He could so easily have come to regard responsibility with a shrugging indifference and taken to a life of indolence and sensuality. In fact he was neither a rake nor a debauchee, nor a drunkard, nor a reckless gambler. On the contrary, he was meticulous in the discharge of his numerous and often onerous duties. But that done, he was entitled, he felt, to the relaxation he had earned, as much as anyone else was. That he was a playboy nobody would attempt to dispute, but his self-indulgence did not reach the excesses of many of his friends and he certainly had far less time to spare than they did. Even though denied the companionship of friends in the classroom and on the playing fields of Eton or any other school, so marked was the stamp of the public school, then as now, that inevitably he absorbed and reflected it like the rest. He admired daring in others and strove to engage in it himself: up to quite late in life he never missed an opportunity of participating in any adventure that demanded courage and a steady nerve. During his visit to Canada, for example, when he was eighteen, he watched Blondin cross the Niagara Falls on a tight-rope with a wheel-barrow. Blondin offered to wheel the Prince across. He was about to accept but was prevented from doing so by those responsible for his safety.[52] In Egypt two years later he climbed to the top of the Great Pyramid 'without assistance and with surprising alacrity'; Napoleon, however, refused quite firmly to undertake it but ordered one of his young lieutenants to do so.

At no time was there any sign of spite or malice in anything Edward did whether as Prince or King. If undue familiarity was shown by any of his friends, as it was by Sir Frederick Johnstone, who while staying at Sandringham called him 'Tum-Tum', a nickname sometimes used behind the stout monarch's back, the King said gently 'Freddy, you're very drunk,' and turning to an equerry told him to make sure that Sir Frederick left the house before breakfast the next morning. But after a time the lapse was forgiven. He was always ready to let bygones be bygones. But he was inclined to be irritable and when roused his temper was terrifying; his closest friends admitted this—his angry bellow (says Ponsonby's daughter, Loelia, Duchess of Westminster) could never be forgotten. But it soon passed and his warm-heartedness prompted him afterwards to make amends.

CHAPTER 6

The New Queen, Alexandra

It was the resolve of both Queen Victoria and Prince Albert that Edward should marry early. The quest for a bride actually began when the Prince was not yet seventeen. A list of possible Princesses was drawn up, all of them German, and was closely studied by the Queen at Windsor and her Uncle Leopold, the King of the Belgians, at Brussels.* But nothing came of it: the Prince was unconcerned and gave his mother a 'confused' reply. Clearly he was not keen on an early marriage. But, apart from reasons of State and the need to make sure of the succession by providing an heir, three years later the marriage seemed to them to be a matter of some urgency. Edward's eldest sister Vicky, who was the wife of Prince Frederick William of Prussia and mother of the future Kaiser Wilhelm II of Germany, was asked to find a bride for her brother. Very low on the initial list of possible brides was the name of Princess Alexandra of Denmark.

Prince Albert was not well disposed to such a marriage. The Princess was at the time only fourteen, but what disturbed Albert was the friction between Denmark and Prussia over the future of the two provinces of Schleswig and Holstein on which Prussia was casting covetous eyes: he did not want England to be involved in any way in the dispute. Alexandra's father, moreover, was an impecunious

* *The Times*, 20th July 1858.

38

officer in the Danish Guards with only £10 a month on which to bring up his family of six children. They lived in a dilapidated house in Copenhagen, known as the Yellow Palace, where Alexandra shared an attic bedroom with her sister Dagmar; there was room in it for only two narrow beds and a chest of drawers. The girls made their own clothes, knitted their own stockings, and waited at table when there were guests, which was not very often. Their mother taught them to play the piano, their father laid stress on outdoor exercise: their main diversion was going for walks, chiefly along the lovely Lange Linie, the famous promenade by the sea. On these walks they often met Hans Christian Andersen and listened with delight to his fairy stories.

Vicky took into her confidence her young and pretty maid-of-honour Walburga, Countess von Hohenthal, who has left a fascinating record of their quest.[45] Various Princesses were inspected at supper parties and receptions in numerous palaces in Germany. It was only after Walburga's marriage to Augustus Paget, the British Minister in Copenhagen, that the name of Princess Alexandra was moved to the top of the list. Wally found the by now seventeen-year-old Princess beautiful, charming and ideally suited to be the future Queen of England. She had delicate features, gentle eyes, a small, attractive mouth and an irresistible smile. Wally wrote enthusiastically about her to Vicky and it was immediately arranged that the Princess should be invited to a friend's house where Vicky could see her. Vicky, in her turn, was enchanted. 'Princess Alix,' she wrote to tell Wally, 'is the most fascinating creature in the world. You did not say nearly enough. For a long time I have seen nobody who pleased me so much as this lovely and charming girl.' She reported this to her father, who eventually approved. After his death, the Queen, although she had not herself met Alexandra, was resolved that her dear Albert's wish should be fulfilled.

Queen Victoria's Uncle Leopold arranged an early meeting. He advised Alexandra to dress very simply and to be careful not to smile, for the Queen, being in mourning, could not bear to see anyone smile. The Queen crossed to Brussels in September 1862 and inspected Alexandra at the palace at Laeken. Wally was present. After the interview the Queen put her head on Wally's shoulder and wept. 'You, dear Wally,' Her Majesty said, 'will quite understand what I feel at this moment. You have a husband you love and you know what I have lost.'[45]

Prince Edward had already seen photographs of Alexandra and had met her twice, as though by chance— the first time in the Cathedral of Speier in Germany, then again at Heidelberg. They hardly spoke, for there were too many relatives about. But the Prince took to her at once. He used to say of her later that she was quite the prettiest lady in London. He was good-looking himself, with pale blue eyes and a slightly cutaway chin, which he concealed later by growing a beard. He was not tall, but stood about four inches above her. Their hair was similar in colour, very light brown with just a tinge of red.

When the Queen gave her approval the Prince said to Wally: 'Now I will walk with Princess Alix in the garden and in three-quarters of an hour I will take her into the Grotto and there I will propose, and I hope it will be to everyone's satisfaction.' There was a much greater depth of feeling than these words, uttered playfully, conveyed. The Prince had been attentive ever since he had first set eyes on her. He bought gifts for her, including some very attractive bracelets from a jeweller in Dresden, who was greatly impressed that the Prince had not troubled even to ask their price. The young man's eagerness was so marked that Uncle Leopold wrote to Queen Victoria: 'The match is quite a love-match. Bertie is extremely happy and in admiration of his very lovely bride. All the arguments that one forced him to marry a young lady that he had never seen, fall to the ground. All this is important, particularly for England, where it will please people very much that the Prince of Wales, like his parents, should marry for affection.'[46]

The wedding took place six months later, on 10th March 1863. The Queen would not hear of having it solemnised at Westminster Abbey, the usual setting for such a ceremony: she was not prepared to go to London and face the crowds. She insisted that it should be held at St George's Chapel at Windsor: it was the first time a royal marriage had been solemnised there for nearly 750 years. Nor was she prepared to give up her widow's weeds even for that one day. She arrived dressed in deep and voluminous mourning and slipped quietly into the gallery above the chancel where she sat unnoticed. Only two things of interest marked the event: Jenny Lind sang in a chorale Prince Albert had composed; and the future Kaiser Wilhelm, then aged four, was there dressed in a kilt; he sat beside Edward's two brothers, Alfred and Leopold, and bit them both in the leg when they tried to stop him throwing his skien dhu across the choir.

There was widespread and scathing criticism of the Queen's decision. The public had been looking forward to a fairy-tale pageantry, with a glass coach and outriders and the Household Cavalry, moving in a slow procession through excited, cheering crowds. For them the event was an utter disappointment. The newspapers were outspokenly denunciatory; *Punch* suggested that the only thing omitted was a brief announcement in the marriage columns of *The Times*, stating that the ceremony had been held in an obscure Berkshire village, noted only for an old castle with no sanitary arrangements.

Nor had the Princess's arrival from Denmark provided any compensation. A thin, miserable and quite unworthy procession, consisting of six carriages and a detachment of Life Guards, progressed from the Bricklayers Arms at Southwark to Paddington station. 'I was never more surprised and disappointed,' records Lord Malmesbury. 'The first five carriages contained the suite and brothers and sisters of the Princess. The carriages looked old and shabby, and the horses very poor, with no trappings, not even rosettes, and no outriders. In short the shabbiness of the whole *cortège* was beyond anything one could imagine.'[47] The Prince sat with the Princess in the sixth carriage.

Marlborough House in Pall Mall had been assigned as a home for the young couple and there the Prince of Wales, aged twenty-one, and his bride, who was three years his junior, began a lively round of entertaining. Both had a great love of gaiety and diversion: it was a bond that drew her and Edward together from the very outset of their marriage. Night after night there were receptions and balls and dinners. This went on for many months and constituted the most extensive honeymoon ever enjoyed by any member of the British Royal family. It met with the sternest disapproval of Queen Victoria, but that did not deter them. The gusto of this hectic social round went on unabated through the succeeding years. The circle of guests was constantly widened. Guests on whose credentials Queen Victoria looked askance were frequently invited. After three years of it the ageing Queen wrote a strong letter to General Knollys, Edward's Comptroller and Treasurer, which she asked him to show to her son. The company, she wrote, had become 'so lax and so bad'; it was their duty, she added, 'to deny themselves amusement, in order to keep up that tone in society which *used* to be the pride of England'. She mentioned in particular 'the fast racing set'. Their manners and their faults, she said, had worsened: her son ought *not* to ask them to dinner, nor have them at Sandringham and above all, he should not visit them in their homes.[44] But of this neither he nor his wife took any notice.

Within a month of his accession the King conferred the Order of the Garter on Queen Alexandra, an unusual honour for a woman who was not herself the sovereign: it was the first time for 400 years that this had been done. All objections were brushed aside by the King, who insisted that, despite the statutes of the Order and precedents, the Queen's banner must be put up with the other Garter banners in St George's Chapel.

Alexandra's sense of fun, her fondness for pranks and practical jokes appealed greatly to Edward, who was very much given to practical joking himself. One day, while her sister Dagmar, mother of Tsar Nicholas II of Russia, was staying at Buckingham Palace and lying ill in bed, Queen Alexandra thought of an amusing charade to divert her. Also staying at the palace at the time was Prince Christopher, the son of her brother Willy, who was by now King George of Greece. Alexandra sent for her nephew. On entering her room, he records,[21] he found that 'on her bed was laid out a miscellaneous collection of mantles, dresses, and bonnets of every description that belonged to Queen Victoria. Queen Alexandra was examining them, her eyes dancing with merriment. "Now, Christo," she said when I came in, "you've got to put this dress on and go down to Aunt Minnie's (the Empress's) room and make her laugh." We chose the dress Queen Victoria had worn in the days of her youth to open the Great Exhibition in Paris under Napoleon III, an alarming creation in tartan taffeta. I struggled into it, perched a befeathered bonnet on my head and added a lace parasol to my costume. Thus attired, I was led by the Queen through endless corridors, past scandalised servants, until we reached the Empress's room, where I was solemnly announced as "Her Majesty Queen Victoria".' The Empress was startled at the apparition, then she was seized with such a violent fit of laughing that she had a serious relapse.

Queen Alexandra, with her modest upbringing, had very simple tastes. She shopped at Liberty's in Regent Street or at Jay's in Oxford Circus, never in Paris: only once was she known to have bought a dress at Worth's. Jean Worth has left a record of this visit: 'She came for the fittings herself . . . and three ladies-in-waiting accompanied her. Alexandra had scarcely stepped on to the tiny stage, to be fitted before these gadflies began: "Don't tire Her Majesty. Be careful of that pin. . . . Watch out now!" The poor fitter dripped with perspiration and trembled with nervousness. . . . Alexandra herself was pleasantly pliant and agreeable to all suggestions.'[49] She was shocked when she learned how much some of her friends paid for their clothes. Daisy, Princess of Pless, arriving at Buckingham Palace in a ball dress of gold tissue and a gold train which cost £400, was chided by her: 'I could not possibly afford such a sum,' she said. The Queen made it clear, adds the Princess of Pless, that it was wicked to pay so much.[50]

Alexandra liked wearing mauves and greys, loved amethysts and especially diamonds which sparkled from her breast and from the deep collar she always wore round her throat. Her passion for music can be traced back to her childhood: her mother had taught her to play the piano well. Going to the opera was a particular joy for her.

She often broke away from routine and did things no member of the Royal family was expected to do. From time to time she went for a walk through the streets of London and was occasionally seen strolling in Berkeley Square with a lady-in-waiting in attendance. They passed unnoticed— hardly a glance was spared for the slight figure dressed in black and the woman beside her.[22] Once, while cruising with the King along the west coast of England, she went for a ride in an electric tram-car. The royal yacht had just arrived at the Isle of Man—no British sovereign had visited the island since Canute, and the King and Queen were quite unexpected. But soon the news was flashed to England and thousands of visitors crossed to the island to see their Majesties.

'We drove to Douglas,' states Sir Frederick Ponsonby,[1] 'where we got into an electric tram and here the fun began. Steamers full of people had been arriving all the afternoon and there must have been four or five thousand people round the tram waving and cheering with no one to keep them back'— for there seemed to be only half a dozen policemen on the whole island.

'A tram, however, is a dangerous thing and the crowd kept at a respectful distance, but when it arrived at the end of its line and we had to get into carriages, the pressure of the crowd was almost frightening. The crowd was so big and so anxious to see the King and Queen that it swept them about in whirlpools. Queen Alexandra had a charming way of treating the crowd as if they were intimate friends, and she was so nervous that people would get hurt that she appealed to those nearest to her to look after the children. The King roared at the coachman to go slowly, but got very cross with him when the carriage stopped, and no one seemed capable of clearing a way, but eventually the carriage got through and arrived at the pier.'

It was the informal, out of the ordinary experiences like these that the Queen enjoyed most, largely because they lay beyond the range of royalty.

One thing that she had in common with Queen Victoria was the love of photographs and souvenirs. Her rooms were full of pictures of relatives, old theatre and opera programmes, bits of ribbon, a fishing fly, and a vast assortment of knick-knacks, most of which she took about with her wherever she went. If the sea got rough during a cruise they were soon scattered about her cabin in dreadful disorder; this must have exasperated the King, but he was tolerant of all her whims and shrugged them off with a smile.

CHAPTER 7

The Scandals

Having excluded her son from taking any part in affairs of State and having, further, expressly instructed her Ministers to withhold from him all official documents, Queen Victoria could hardly expect Edward to occupy his time in any way other than with frivolity and diversion. The only contribution she allowed him to make in public affairs was the laying of foundation stones and the opening of bazaars. That had been his lot for many years. Later, through his own seeking, he sat on committees to promote social welfare, and in time, as the inevitability of his accession drew near, he was able to persuade a few of her Ministers to pass on to him secretly some of the State papers, in particular those dealing with foreign affairs.

The old Queen was said to have nursed the secret fear that, like the heirs of the earlier Georges, her son too might have been used as the rallying point of a clique opposed to the Court. But no mother could have had a more loyal son: not for one moment would he have countenanced, let alone encouraged, any critic. That there were many critics Victoria knew only too well. Anger and disgust at the Queen's complete detachment from public life were widespread. But as her attention to affairs of State never slackened and she sat up far into the night, alone in the privacy of her room, poring over endless ministerial documents, she regarded any comment on her withdrawal as a heartless and irresponsible persecution, and insisted that she was entitled to the sympathy of her subjects. There was a growing feeling among people, even in high places and in responsible positions, that the Queen should abdicate. On 4th June 1864, little more than a year after Edward's marriage, Lord Howden, a prominent and experienced diplomatist, wrote to Lord Clarendon, a member of Palmerston's Government, that the Queen would have done well in view of 'the turn of her mind from the beginning of her widowhood, to abdicate the day her son came of age.'[5]

The Queen had no intention of being influenced in any way by such talk. When at last, a year or so later, she did hold a Drawing Room and drove through Hyde Park afterwards, she made a point of writing to her Uncle Leopold in Belgium to make it quite clear how much more popular she was than her son, even when he had the lovely Princess Alexandra beside him: 'Everyone said that the difference shown, when *I* appeared and (when) Bertie and Alix drive, was *not* to be described. Naturally for *them* no-one stops, or *runs*, as they always did, and *do* doubly now, for *me*.'[2] The jealousy is, of course, unmistakable, and there is also the latent criticism of those who were foolish enough to imagine that her son would be an adequate substitute for her. It was her answer to the call for abdication.

She clung to the view her husband had always held, that Bertie was not very intelligent. The ministerial papers were withheld from him, she said, because he was indiscreet. As an example she cited her son's attitude when at last Prussia attacked Denmark for the possession of the disputed provinces of Schleswig-Holstein. Albert had always said that Denmark had no right to the provinces. What business then was it of Bertie's to show his sympathy for his wife's country and to take sides against his own sister, who was married to the heir of the King of Prussia? Then again when Garibaldi, who had been largely instrumental in uniting Italy, visited England as the Duke of Sutherland's guest, Bertie ought not to have gone to see him since, technically, Garibaldi was a rebel.

Moreover, some of his dissolute friends had got him into the most embarrassing scrapes. The Mordaunt divorce case was an instance. In 1869, when Bertie had been married for six years and already had five children, the public was startled to learn that the Heir to the Throne was to be involved in the case. The Prince was then twenty-eight years old.

Sir Charles Mordaunt, a wealthy young baronet, only recently married to the very lovely Harriet Moncrieffe, whose sister was one of the Queen's ladies-in-waiting, had disapproved of her friendship with the Prince of Wales.

Harriet's family lived on an estate adjoining Balmoral and the Prince had known her since she was a girl; she was now twenty-one. Before her marriage she had been a guest of the Prince and Princess of Wales at Marlborough House, but her husband, jealous and possessive, had asked her to discontinue her friendship with the Prince. In temperament Sir Charles and Lady Mordaunt were ill-matched. He was staid and serious in disposition, she lively and amusing. There had been two miscarriages since the marriage and, though frail in health, she had insisted on continuing her gay social round. Her husband told her many damaging things about the Prince, but it had no effect and he found that they were still seeing each other.

Trouble started with the premature birth of her first child, a girl weighing only three and a half pounds and seemingly blind. In the hysteria of her distress, Lady Mordaunt, it was stated in court, confessed to her husband that she had deceived him. 'You are not the father of that child,' she said. 'I am the cause of its blindness . . . I have been very wicked. I have done very wrong.'

'Who with?' he asked.

'With Lord Cole, Sir Frederick Johnstone, the Prince of Wales, and others,' she said. Lord Cole and Sir Frederick Johnstone were close friends of the Prince. She hinted that Lord Cole was the father of the child.

Sir Charles, wondering if there could be any truth in her wild outburst, began to search for corroboration and found

Queen Victoria's funeral

Prince Albert, the Prince Consort

Baron Stockmar

King Edward aged four (standing) with two of his sisters. From a drawing by Queen Victoria

'The rare, the rather awful visits of Albert Edward, Prince of Wales, to Windsor Castle.' From *Things Old and New* by Max Beerbohm

Above The Young Prince Edward (standing), with his tutors at Oxford

Below Prince Edward and Princess Alexandra with Queen Victoria on their wedding day

Edward and Alexandra with their first child, Albert Victor, later Duke of Clarence

Below Princess Alexandra, Princess of Wales

Tsar Nicholas II of
Russia and the Tsaritsa

Sir Ernest Cassel

Above. 'Are we as welcome as ever?' From *Fifty Caricatures* by Max Beerbohm

Below Sir William Gordon-Cumming

Above Lord Charles Beresford

Below Lord Randolph Churchill

in a locked desk a valentine sent to her by the Prince, one of his handkerchiefs and eleven letters written to her by him.

Despite this the Prince was not cited as a co-respondent, but it was clear when the case opened in 1870 that Sir Charles Mordaunt's counsel, Sergeant Ballantyne, was not going to let him off lightly. Referring to her statement 'I have done very wrong', Ballantyne said: 'I will show that these words were true as regards her conduct with that gentleman. Her husband had objected to her keeping up an acquaintance with that gentleman and had no knowledge that she continued that acquaintance. I shall produce a number of letters from the gentleman himself, not indicating actual crime, but showing that improper correspondence took place.'

The butler and lady's maid stated in their evidence that the Prince had called on Lady Mordaunt when she was staying at the Alexandra Hotel in London, arriving at four in the afternoon and not leaving until half past five or six, that he did not on such occasions use his private carriage, and that Lady Mordaunt had given strict instructions that no one else was to be admitted while the Prince was there.

The question was now raised whether Lady Mordaunt was fit to plead and the defence argued that she was unable to do so because of her insanity; but her husband's counsel insisted that she was in her senses when she made her confession and was only simulating madness now. He argued, however, that he was not in a position to contradict the evidence that had been brought forward as to the *present* state of her mind.

This was a victory for the defence to which both Lord Cole and Sir Frederick Johnstone were a party as co-respondents.

A provincial newspaper managed to get hold of the eleven letters written by the Prince to Lady Mordaunt and published them. They were friendly notes, using such phrases as 'The Princess has a little girl and both are doing well', and 'I hope when I come back from Paris to make the acquaintance of your husband'. There were also references

49

to shooting and hunting and the royal children's measles. These letters were later published in 'An Official Report' of the trial

The Prince was subpoenaed as a witness by Sergeant Ballantyne. This caused the utmost distress to Queen Victoria. But the Prince decided to waive his plea of privilege, and, after discussing it with the Lord Chancellor, Lord Heatherley, he went into the witness box on 23rd February 1870. He was examined by Dr Deane, Lady Mordaunt's counsel, and 'in a very firm tone' denied that there had been any improper familiarity or criminal act between him and Lady Mordaunt. He was in the box for seven minutes altogether. Immediately afterwards he wrote to his mother: 'I trust that by what I have said today the public at large will be satisfied that the gross imputations which have been so wantonly cast upon me are now cleared up.'[5]

But the public were not in fact satisfied. Edward was greeted with hisses when he arrived at the theatre and when he appeared on the racecourse at Epsom; even when the Princess of Wales was with him at the Crystal Palace the crowd expressed its disapproval in the same way. At other times he was received in absolute silence.[7] *The Times* chided him in a leading article and advised him to follow in his father's footsteps. Other newspapers took up the theme. There was talk of abolishing the monarchy and setting up a republic, since the cost of maintaining the Crown was too high. Gladstone, Prime Minister at the time, warned the Prince that 'so long as the nation has confidence in the personal character of its sovereign the throne of this Empire may be regarded as secure'; and the Lord Chancellor told him that the Prince of Wales was expected to set a strict example.

Sir Charles Mordaunt's petition for divorce was dismissed on the ground that his wife's mental condition disabled her from being a party to the suit. It was not until five years later that divorce was at last granted.

In the course of the succeeding years two further scandals

followed. Among the Prince's friends were three very attractive American girls known as the Jerome sisters, the eldest of whom, Jennie, married Lord Randolph Churchill in 1874 and thus became Winston Churchill's mother. The Prince of Wales's secretary, Sir Francis Knollys, was best man at their wedding, which took place in the British Embassy in Paris. The scandal did not directly concern the three sisters, but it led to a break in the Prince's friendship with the Churchills.

The trouble began in the autumn of 1875 when the Prince set out on an official tour of India. Queen Victoria had been strongly against the tour. She did not like Bertie representing her and gave a variety of evasive reasons, but Disraeli, then Prime Minister, was persistent and in the end she agreed.

She next objected to some of the young men who were to accompany the Prince. Among these was the Earl of Aylesford, to whose pretty wife Edith the Prince had once been paying a great deal of attention, but there was no suggestion of Lady Aylesford also being on the tour. Her husband, known to his friends as 'Sporting Joe', was regarded as one of the best riders in England and the Prince was taking him along for the polo and the pig-sticking.

Shortly after Aylesford left, Lord Blandford, Lord Randolph Churchill's elder brother and heir to the Duke of Marlborough, moved his horses for the hunting season to an inn near Lady Aylesford's country house. A buzz of gossip began and spread rapidly. Blandford's interest in pretty women was well known. He had often been compared with his grandfather, the sixth Duke of Marlborough, who in his eagerness to seduce a Miss Susan Law had got a friend in the Guards to dress up as a parson and perform the marriage ceremony. A great many children were born without Miss Law discovering that the marriage was bogus. When she learned the truth, the weeping victim was given an annuity and the Duke married the daughter of the Earl of Galloway.

It was inevitable that the news of Blandford's present *liaison* should reach India. Aylesford heard of it not only

51

from friends, but presently a letter arrived from his wife to say that she and Blandford were about to elope.

Aylesford showed the letter to the Prince, whose sympathies were entirely with the wronged husband. He described Blandford as 'the greatest blackguard alive'. Granted leave, Aylesford promptly left the Prince's party and hurried home to start divorce proceedings.

It was at this point that Lord Randolph Churchill (known as 'Gooseberry face') intervened on behalf of his brother. He sent a telegram to the Prince to ask him to persuade Aylesford not to bring the divorce action. The Prince refused to interfere; no one had any right, he declared, to interfere in Aylesford's private life.

Determined to prevent the widespread scandal that divorce would have caused at that time, Lord Randolph put family pressure on Blandford not to elope. He then called on Lady Aylesford. As an aid to the persuasion of the Prince, he managed to get hold of some indiscreet letters which the Prince had once written to her. There was some doubt as to how he had got the letters. It was believed that he climbed through a window into the lady's house and stole them, but she was said later to have given Blandford the letters. These letters were described by the Marquess of Hartington, heir of the Duke of Devonshire and an intimate friend of the Prince, as being 'written in a strain of undue familiarity and containing many foolish and somewhat stupid expressions.'[44] There was no doubt that their publication would injure the reputation of the Prince, and Lord Randolph chuckled as he told his friends boastfully that he had the Crown of England in his pocket.

In order to blackmail the Prince into submission with a view to stopping the divorce, Randolph, while the Prince was still away on his tour, called on the Princess of Wales at Marlborough House. He told her of the letters and warned her that he would use every means in his power to gain his end. If these compromising letters were to be published, he said, the Prince 'would never sit upon the Throne of England'.

The Princess was naturally very deeply distressed. News of the interview was sent to the Prince and reached him at Cairo while he was on his way home. He was furious. He wrote to his friend the Earl of Hardwicke to keep an eye on developments and to discuss the situation secretly with the Prime Minister, Disraeli.

At the same time he sent home his *aide-de-camp*, the breezy young Irish naval lieutenant Lord Charles Beresford,* instructing him to call on Lord Randolph and challenge him to a duel. Pistols were suggested and the encounter was to be somewhere on the north coast of France or at Rotterdam. Lady Randolph Churchill, the dark, lovely Jennie Jerome, who had been an intimate of the Marlborough House set, was greatly disturbed. Her 'iron nerves', we are told by her great-niece,[9] 'began to grow frayed'. She passed sleepless nights until Randolph appointed Lord Falmouth as his second and despatched him with a message to say that he would fight any nominee of the Prince's, but not his future Sovereign.

On his return to England the Prince minced no words about Blandford's behaviour and, according to Lady Randolph's side of the family, insisted that Blandford should seek a divorce from his own wife and do the right thing by marrying Lady Aylesford.[9]

The duel was not fought. Lord Randolph, his wife writes, 'felt in need of solace and distraction', so they left hastily for Canada with their two-year-old son, Winston.

But the Prince was still angry and made it quite clear that he would not set foot in any house that continued to receive the Churchills. As a consequence the ostracism was complete. The Duke of Marlborough left to become Viceroy of Ireland. Lord Randolph and his wife, whose life ever since their marriage had been filled with 'gaieties and festivities', as their son describes it in the biography of his father, spent the years that followed in social exile.[9] Winston Churchill, writing of this in 1905 (the book was published in 1907 when

* Lord Charles' quarrel with the King did not occur until many years later.

53

Edward the Seventh was on the throne), says: 'Engaging in his brother's quarrels with fierce and reckless partisanship, Lord Randolph incurred the deep displeasure of a great personage. The fashionable world no longer smiled. Powerful enemies were anxious to humiliate him. His own sensitiveness and pride magnified every coldness into an affront. London became odious to him. The breach was not repaired for more than eight years, and in the interval a nature originally genial and gay contracted a stern and bitter quality, a harsh contempt for what is called "Society", and an abiding antagonism to rank and authority. If this misfortune produced in Lord Randolph characteristics which afterwards hindered or injured his public work, it was also a spur.' The House of Commons had been 'but one among various diversions', but he began now to apply himself more diligently to his political career.[10]

Let us look for a moment at the others involved in this unsavoury affair. Aylesford, in order to avoid a public scandal in which the Prince would have figured, abandoned his intention of divorcing his wife. She left him, however, and lived in Paris with Lord Blandford for many years as Mr and Mrs Spencer, "Spencer' being part of the family name of Spencer-Churchill. In the late seventies, Aylesford decided to divorce his wife after all. The case was started, but the Queen's Proctor intervened and revealed that Aylesford had been carrying on a succession of 'vulgar amours' with women of the lowest type. Finally in 1883 Lady Blandford divorced her husband and that was when it emerged that he had been living in Paris with Lady Aylesford. All the men involved had been close personal friends of the Prince of Wales.

The third was a very different kind of scandal. It arose from a game of baccarat at which one of the guests was accused of cheating. This occurred at Tranby Croft, near Doncaster, the home of a wealthy shipowner named Arthur Wilson, yet another of the Prince's industrial friends of whom Queen Victoria so strongly disapproved. Throughout her reign immense fortunes were being made by such men by spreading all over the country a network of railways, the new mode of transport, or from the conversion of sailing ships to steam, the building of numerous factories or from finding fresh markets far afield for the products of other people's factories. With their wealth they had bought famous country houses or had built new ones on large estates, houses that were not always as impressively elegant as the houses of the preceding century, for the new furniture was massive and room had always to be found for a billiard table. Though looked down on as *nouveau riche*, these were in fact the emergent aristocracy of traders, who had readily received the royal seal of recognition in the reign of Queen Elizabeth the First. Queen Victoria had confined her circle to royal relatives from Europe and a very few members of the old nobility. Of the English aristocracy as a whole Prince Albert had the poorest opinion, since they had been responsible, he felt, for the Queen leading such a gay and frivolous life during her first years on the throne. To draw into the social circle industrialists, lawyers and doctors, Americans and Jews, as her son had done, and to substitute laughter and sport for serious conversation, caused her the acutest distress. This oppressive, confining, critical attitude at the top, engendered by her widowed seclusion, kept the younger, brighter world of her son completely beyond the pale.

A number of guests had been invited by Wilson to stay at Tranby Croft for the Doncaster races, which were to be held on 8th and 9th September 1890. Among them were the Prince of Wales, Lord Coventry, General Owen Williams, Lord Edward Somerset, and Sir William Gordon-Cumming, all of them friends of the Prince; also staying in the house were various members of the host's family.

The Prince was forty-eight at the time. He had always been fond of gambling and had played at casinos in Germany and on the French Riviera. The Press, alluding to such visits in their gossip columns, often accused him of wagering recklessly. The Prince denied this.[11] At any rate the baccarat played by the house party at Tranby Croft was for comparatively low stakes.

55

The incident, which led later to a law suit, occurred on the very first evening of the Prince's stay. He held the bank that night and the counters, which he had brought with him, represented various values from five shillings to £10.

The game had not long been in progress when Mr A. S. Wilson, the twenty-two-year-old son of the host, thought he saw his neighbour at the table, Sir William Gordon-Cumming, cheating. He whispered this to the man on his other side, Mr Berkeley Levett, who was one of Gordon-Cumming's junior officers. Both then watched and both saw him cheating again. The three tables placed together for the game were of unequal height and Gordon-Cumming was seen, under cover of his hand, to be withdrawing or augmenting his stakes according to the value of his cards; at one point the Prince of Wales was heard to say to Gordon-Cumming: 'I wish you would put your stakes where they can be seen.'

Wilson later mentioned it to his mother, but not to his father, who objected to the younger generation playing baccarat. The next morning Mr Lycett Green, a Master of Foxhounds and brother-in-law of young Wilson, was also told and so was his wife. There were thus four members of the Wilson family who knew, in addition to Berkeley Levett.

It was arranged that the game should be played again the next evening and that a proper table should be used so that it would be possible to see exactly what was going on. Nine sat down to play. Four of them, including the Prince, were unaware of the suspicions. Once again the Prince was the banker.

Young Green saw Gordon-Cumming cheating again. He was about to get up and denounce the man, but in order to avoid a scene scribbled a note to his mother-in-law instead. Young Wilson, his mother and his sister had also noticed it, but the fifth in the know had refused to look in the direction of his senior officer.

The four met later, discussed the matter, and decided to tell three of the remaining players—Lord Coventry, Lord Edward Somerset and General Owen Williams. The general was a close friend of Gordon-Cumming's. Only the Prince was not told.

These three seemed to feel that Gordon-Cumming must be guilty and decided to place the matter before the Prince.

Together with General Williams, the Prince questioned the five witnesses and then saw Gordon-Cumming, who insisted that he was innocent. But the Prince maintained that the weight of evidence was against him. A document was then drawn up for Gordon-Cumming to sign, in which he promised that he would never play cards again for money.

The paper was also signed by the eight other players as witnesses, the Prince's signature heading the list, and by two others who had not been party to the game. The document was then sent by the Prince to his secretary to be filed among his private papers.

The witnessing signatories in their turn promised that not a word of the affair would be disclosed to anyone outside the group. All the others in the house, including such prominent guests as Lady Londonderry and the Prince's equerry, Mr Christopher Sykes, were left completely ignorant of what had happened.

Sir William Gordon-Cumming left the next morning and there the matter would appear to have ended. But it didn't. Gossip got about. People began to cut Gordon-Cumming. He received an anonymous letter and wrote to General Owen Williams to say that somebody must have talked, but was assured that all had remained as silent as the grave.

There is in existence a letter, dated 1st April 1891, from the Prince to Mrs Arthur Paget in which he says: 'Well can I understand how shocked Arthur was at the news of his Brother Officer. . . . Perhaps you would ascertain from your French friend when he played B. at Paris since Sept. last.' This appears to refer to Gordon-Cumming and it seems to suggest that he had played baccarat. Possibly that was why some of the others no longer felt obliged to remain silent.

Gordon-Cumming decided that, since so many knew, something would have to be done, and he brought a suit for slander against the five original accusers, four of whom were members of the Wilson family, the fifth a subaltern in his own regiment.

The case opened on 1st June 1891. It was heard before the Lord Chief Justice, Lord Coleridge, and lasted seven days. The Prince sat in the court for the entire time.

Gordon-Cumming denied his guilt. When asked why he had signed the document, he said he was prepared to make any personal sacrifice in order that the Prince's name should be kept out of the affair.

When the Prince, who had been subpoenaed, stepped into the witness box to give evidence, he seemed most reluctant to do so.[5] He narrated what he knew of the affair. Under cross-examination he admitted that he had had a long and close friendship with Gordon-Cumming. Just as he was stepping down a juryman asked His Royal Highness: 'I understand you saw no foul play?'

'It is difficult for the banker to see the play,' the Prince replied, 'and moreover at the house of a friend you are not likely to expect foul play.'

'What was your opinion at the time as to the charges made?' asked the juryman.

'They seemed so strongly supported,' said the Prince, 'unanimously so—by those who brought them forward, that I felt that no other course was open to me but to believe what I was told.'

The verdict of the jury went against Gordon-Cumming and he was ordered to pay costs.

The moment the case ended the floodgates opened for widespread criticism of the Prince's way of life. Noncomformists held meetings all over the country and were quite unrestrained in their attack. The Welsh Baptists denounced his 'immoral habits'. The Weslyans 'bitterly regretted that the Heir to the Throne should be given to one of the worst forms of gambling . . . and that he took about with him counters for the game.' *The Times* 'almost wished for the sake of English society' that the Prince would follow the example of Sir William Gordon-Cumming and sign a declaration that he would never touch a card again. The *Review of Reviews*, estimating that 880 million prayers had been said for His Royal Highness since his birth, indicated that the only answer from the Almighty seemed to be a baccarat scandal. The 'Wee Frees' removed the Prince's name from their prayers. When he arrived to open a new hall in Camberwell he was met with a banner inscribed: 'Welcome to our Prince—but No Gambling.'

In the House of Commons on 15th June, a few days after the case ended, attention was called to the Prince's breach of the Queen's Regulations, No. 41, which directed that all officers on the active list suspecting a fellow officer of dishonourable conduct must submit the case to his commanding officer. The Prince had taken the matter into his own hands and had made Gordon-Cumming atone for his offence by a private confession. Through the Secretary of State for War the Prince admitted to the House 'an error of judgement'.

Nowhere in the world was he spared. The American press, the newspapers on the Continent, the cartoonists all joined in. One German paper, in a cartoon, showed the great door of Windsor Castle decorated with the Prince of Wales' feathers, but the familiar motto was altered from "Ich Dien' (I serve) to 'Ich Deal'. The Prince also received a rebuke from his nephew the Kaiser, who in a personal letter expressed his displeasure that anyone holding the high position of Colonel in the Prussian Huzzars should 'embroil himself in a gambling squabble and play with men young enough to be his sons.'

Queen Victoria was acutely distressed. She wrote to her son again and again: they were sharp, scolding letters. She asked him to give up playing cards, and eventually extracted the promise that he would never again allow baccarat to be played in his presence. A drawing made at about this time by Max Beerbohm, shows the Queen looking extremely grave and sad; in a corner of the room, with his face to the wall, stands the plump, ageing Prince, like a naughty schoolboy. The caption reads: 'The rare, the rather awful visits of Albert Edward, Prince of Wales, to Windsor Castle.'

The Prince, disturbed by the public outcry and the anguish it was causing the Queen, invited the Archbishop of Canterbury, Dr E. W. Benson, to come and see him at Marlborough House. He began the interview by asking bluntly if the

Archbishop had inspired the fierce attacks in the Church newspapers condemning him 'as a gambler and worse'.

The Archbishop said there was no truth whatsoever in the accusation. He had been most careful not to write or say a word about the affair, in fact any discussion of it was forbidden in his own house. But if the Prince would like to know what he thought of it he would be glad to tell him.

An account of this discussion was later published by the Archbishop's son E. F. Benson.[12] The Prince stated emphatically that he was not a gambler, but saw no harm in it in moderation. He would never try to put down betting, he said—it was a national instinct and every small boy in a grocer's shop put his sixpence on the Derby. 'There's no harm in playing cards for money in itself,' he went on. 'One of the first men I ever played cards with was Bishop Wilberforce.'

The Prince put his point of view even more explicitly in a letter to the Archbishop dated 13th August 1891. He wrote: 'A recent trial which no one deplores more than I do and which I was powerless to prevent, gave occasion for the Press to make most bitter and unjust attacks upon me, knowing that I was defenceless, and I am not sure that politics were not mixed up in it. The whole matter has now died down, and I think therefore it would be inopportune for me in any public manner to allude again to the painful subject which brought such a torrent of abuse upon me not only by the Press, but by the Low Church and especially the Nonconformists.

'They have a perfect right, as I am well aware, in a free country like our own to express their opinions, but I do not consider they have a just right to jump at conclusions regarding myself without knowing the facts.

'I have a horror of gambling and should always do my utmost to discourage others who have no inclination for it, as I consider that gambling, like intemperance, is one of the greatest curses which a country can be afflicted with.

'Horse-racing may produce gambling or it may not, but I have always looked upon it as a manly sport which is popular with Englishmen of all classes, and there is no reason why it should be looked upon as a gambling transaction. Alas! Those who gamble will gamble at anything.'

In the years following the Tranby Croft case the rumour got about that Gordon-Cumming had cheated deliberately in order to divert the attention of the other players from the Prince whom he had caught cheating. This rumour was eventually given expression in print in a book written by J. A. Frere, a former Chester Herald at Arms.[13] He claims that the ninth Lord Middleton, who was married to Gordon-Cumming's sister Eliza, was offered an earldom as a reward for such self-sacrificing loyalty but refused it on his wife's insistence. His brother, the tenth baron, far less closely connected with Gordon-Cumming, was next offered an earldom and also refused it, but eventually in 1957 the eleventh baron was made a Knight of the Garter. 'The Crown has a very long memory,' wrote Frere, 'and *noblesse oblige*.' Lord Middleton was furious when he read this. 'Absolute poppycock,' he said angrily. 'Pure moonshine! To suggest that I was made a Knight of the Garter because of a scandal that happened seventy years ago is sheer nonsense.'

If such a reward were to be given it might have been more justly conferred on the direct descendants of Gordon-Cumming, who married an American heiress shortly after the case: they had two sons and two daughters. His home at Gordonstoun in Scotland later became a school, at which the present Prince of Wales, great-great-grandson of King Edward the Seventh, is a boarder.

These scandals brought no alteration in the Prince's mode of life. He continued to attend race-meetings, to spend long week-ends at the country houses of his *nouveau-riche* friends (accompanied often by his wife), and to go about with beautiful women. Many criticised his conduct, but there were vast numbers of others who rejoiced that the Heir to the Throne, should, without impairing his dignity, have abandoned hypocrisy and humbug and identified himself with their own diversions—in short that he was 'one of them'.

CHAPTER 8

The King's Finances

It was expected on the King's accession that, as with George the Fourth, his finances would be heavily burdened with debt. Parliament appointed the customary commission to examine the position: its three members were Mr A. J. Balfour, Leader of the House of Commons, Sir William Harcourt, a former member of Gladstone's Liberal Government, and Sir John Blundell Maple, a business friend of the King's.

Into the sombre committee room walked the King's Private Secretary, Sir Francis (not yet Lord) Knollys. Bowing as he took his seat, he said: 'Gentlemen, it is my happy duty to inform you that, for the first time in English history, the heir-apparent comes forward to claim his right to the throne unencumbered by a single penny of debt.'[5]

Edward was by no means as extravagant as many seemed to suppose. Although he entertained lavishly at Marlborough House and Sandringham, kept racehorses, travelled extensively and always dressed immaculately, he took good care to see that his expenditure was kept well within bounds. In addition he was admirably served by Sir Ernest Cassel and other friends in the City, such as the Rothschilds and Baron Hirsch, who assisted him with his investments.

The Duchy of Cornwall, which is always reserved for the use of the heir-apparent, brought in about £60,000 a year. During his minority this income had been handled most prudently by his father and Edward found on coming of age that he had a capital sum of £600,000. Out of this he bought Sandringham for £220,000 and spent a further £100,000 on furniture, carriages and jewellery. Sandringham proved a good investment, for the rent roll from this 7,000-acre estate amounted to nearly £7,000 a year. In addition he received as Prince of Wales a Parliamentary grant of £40,000 a year, making an annual total of approximately £100,000—barely a third of the income most of his friends enjoyed.

The allowance to be paid to him as King had now to be considered. His Majesty made it clear at the outset that he was resolved on introducing economies in his Household. It was nearly half a century, he said, since the Royal Household and its administration had been overhauled, and he urged that to begin with the salaries of the Parliamentary members of his Household should be reduced from £10,700 a year to £7,700, and that there should also be a reduction in the salaries of future Treasurers, Comptrollers and Vice-Chamberlains. He further caused considerable dismay by approving the reduction of the number of Lords-in-Waiting from eight to six.

The Chancellor of the Exchequer, Sir Michael Hicks-Beach, appointed an investigating committee in March 1901 to go into these proposals and decide finally what the income of the new King and Queen and other members of the royal family should be. The committee consisted of twenty-three members, drawn from all political parties in the House. Queen Victoria had been receiving £385,000 a year, on which no income tax was paid. The recurrent complaint had been that she had never spent anything like that sum, but while living in retirement had been saving the money like a miser: it was believed by many that she was the richest woman in Europe. As King Edward's mode of life would obviously be different, it was arranged that his allowance should be increased to £470,000 a year, with £70,000 a year for Queen Alexandra in the event of her becoming a widow. In addition sums were voted by Parliament for pensions, the repair of the palaces, and the upkeep of the royal yachts. The repair and upkeep of Sandringham was a personal liability. Edward inherited not a penny from Queen Victoria: her entire vast fortune went to her younger children. Thus to keep out of debt Edward had to rely on his investments and the income of £60,000 a year he now received from the Duchy of Lancaster. There were moments of embarrassment when he had to draw on what was left of his capital and even in the past to borrow money, but that was before the advice of Cassel and his other financier friends began to bring in an ample harvest.

His Majesty had the privilege of franking letters and sending telegrams free of charge on all State business. The Parliamentary grant, it was agreed, should remain unaltered throughout the King's reign. An attempt by the Treasury to adjust it in 1907, shortly after the Liberals came into power, was immediately challenged by the King. It had been the practice of the State to bear the expense of all official visits by crowned heads, he said, and the suggestion that His Majesty should himself meet these costs in future brought a sharp note from Lord Knollys, the Royal secretary. 'The King will not give in on this point,' he wrote, 'and if it is persisted in I hope His Majesty immediately on his return will send for the Prime Minister and tell him he will not stand such an attempted evasion by the Treasury of what was agreed upon in 1901.'

The Liberal Government, with Asquith as Chancellor of the Exchequer, finally gave way, but introduced the proviso that the Secretary of State for Foreign Affairs should decide which of the visits by crowned heads were of national importance. Even to this the King objected most vehemently. 'As I understand it,' wrote Lord Knollys, 'the Secretary of State for Foreign Affairs would decide what visits were of "political importance" and what not, and the Treasury would only pay for the former. His Majesty has, however, his own views respecting the importance, from a political point of view, of visits of Foreign Sovereigns to this country, which might not coincide with those of the Secretary of State. . . . If the proposal in question were, therefore, to be carried into effect, there might be constant conflicts between the King on one side and the Treasury and the Foreign Office on the other. Altogether independent, however, of this objection there remains the principle that an agreement is an agreement, and I know the King will regard it as being very unfair that there should be any attempt to disturb it especially after it has been in existence for upwards of six years.'

The firm, unyielding attitude of the King led to the Government abandoning their proposal, and the arrangement was left undisturbed until the end of the reign. Thus even in this was His Majesty able to assert himself.

No monarch has since exercised quite the same authority. Queen Victoria, despite her recurrent rages and her continuous criticism of such ministers as Gladstone, had to yield in the end; King Edward, on the other hand, recognised the hazards and knew how far he could go in asserting his constitutional rights. He realised that the trump card was always held by his ministers who, in any conflict with the King, had the effective weapon of resignation. The fiction preserved in the official phrasing that all State appointments and all honours are the prerogative of the Sovereign veils politely the authority that is employed solely by the Prime Minister with the aid of a committee of his own choosing, known as the Cabinet. With all such decisions the Sovereign must abide. 'He must sign,' as Bagehot has said, 'his own death warrant if the two Houses unanimously send it up to him.' Influence can be exerted, and is still, and King Edward had to use his with the utmost firmness and skill in an acute crisis that arose towards the close of his reign.

CHAPTER 9

Country House Parties

The King's week-end visits to his friends often took him away from the famous towered, castellated or palladian mansions; many of them were newly-built residences with hideous echoes of the architecture of St Pancras railway station; but they all possessed the glitter and opulence that were the mark of that ostentatious and extravagant age.

Every week-end the entertainment in these country houses was lavish and profuse, far more so when the King happened to be a guest. The expense in some cases proved to be ruinous, and it was said that some of the King's friends brought themselves to the verge of bankruptcy as a result. Often as many as fifty guests arrived for the week-end. They came as a rule on Friday afternoon. It was not the jaunty affair that it has since become. One did not set off with a suit-case or two and the family piled into the car. These gatherings were strictly for grown-ups. The motor-car, still something of an adventure, was hardly used at all at the beginning of the Edwardian age. The guests came as a rule by train. Outside the station an assortment of carriages waited—large landaus, victorias, wagonettes, dog-carts, buggies, traps and flys, as well as sturdy waggons equipped with wooden seats for the servants and the baggage, for every man brought his valet, every woman her ladies' maid; and since clothes were changed three or four times each day by men, who came with tweeds, sporting jackets, jodhpurs, lounge suits, dinner jackets and evening clothes, and women with their lovely dresses of silk and sateen and velvet as well as evening gowns by Worth and Lucile, the quantity of luggage—trunks, hat boxes, dressing cases, jewel boxes, shoe boxes, gun cases, Wellingtons, parasols and umbrellas—was formidable.

Thus they would set out in a cavalcade along the country roads, passing horse drays, bicycles mounted by men or women, riders on horseback, but only rarely a motor-car, which was usually at a standstill with the 'engineer' tinkering with the works or feeding the radiator with water ('drinks more than a horse', some rustic wit never failed to shout). The cavalcade clattered and jingled along with a cloud of dust in its wake, the horses puffing, snorting and littering the roadway with manure, the coachmen *whoa*-ing, the ladies' maids giggling and jesting with the valets and grooms.

Arrived at the house, the guests, after being welcomed in the hall by the hostess, were escorted to their rooms, most of which already had their names upon the doors. It had been a matter of very careful planning, Mr So-and-so having to be near, or not too near, the pretty Countess of X. The resident servants dealt with the accommodation for the visiting valets and maids—on an average three servants were brought by every guest and each servant was accorded the deference due to the rank and status of the employer. The King came with a gentleman-in-waiting and two equerries, a valet, his own horses and two grooms if it was in the hunting season, two loaders and his own dogs when he came for the shooting.

At five o'clock tea would be served in the pink drawing-room or at one end of the long gallery. There would be scones and cucumber sandwiches, chocolate cake and possibly also ginger biscuits, of which every hostess kept a store because King Edward had become very fond of them while in Biarritz. Lobster salad was also served at tea if the King was there.

Meanwhile trunks would be unpacked, the clothes would be set out for dinner, and baths would be turned on—not many baths for there were few bathrooms in the old houses and one always had to walk to the end of the corridor to reach them. A fire was lit in every bedroom, for summer was over and the season had ended in London. After tea came bridge: and some of the men went off to play billiards for an hour or so.

Dinner was at half past eight. The ladies got out of their tea gowns, altered their hair style, held their breath to get into their corsets, then put on one of their loveliest evening gowns, and spent some time selecting the right necklaces, brooches and rings: then picking up the appropriate ostrich feather fan (no evening bags) they went downstairs.

Looking back on these country house parties, the ladies of the Edwardian decade confessed with a sigh that a large part of their time was spent on dressing and undressing. 'We were for ever changing our clothes,' says Lady Cynthia Asquith.[36] 'Winter was the worst season for changing. You came down to breakfast in your "best dress", usually made of velvet, and after Church changed into tweeds. Another "change" was made for tea—those who possessed that special creation into a tea-gown; the less affluent into a summer day-dress. However small your dress allowance, a different dinner gown was considered essential for each evening. Thus a Friday to Monday party involved taking your "Sunday Best", two tweed coats and skirts, three garments suitable for tea, your "best hat"—usually a vast affair loaded with feathers, fruit or corn—a variety of country headgear, as likely as not a billycock hat and a riding habit, numerous accessories in the way of petticoats, stoles, scarves, evening wreaths and what not; and a large bag in which to carry about the house your embroidery—then the most universal "work" of the idle, for "reading aloud, that gentle entertainment now all but killed" by wireless and television, was still much in vogue, and while one member of the house-party read nearly all the Shes would ply their needles.'

No reading aloud when the King was there: he did not care for it. If the weather was fine and he wasn't out shooting or motoring (which he found a delightful diversion), he enjoyed playing croquet with the ladies. Once at Sir Ernest Cassel's the attractive Duchess of Sermoneta was asked to join the game, but she had heard that the King hated losing and she tried to get out of it. In the end she was persuaded. As she had hardly ever played and kept on missing the hoops, the King was delighted. But when, through complete indifference, she writes,[37] she hit her ball hard and 'it flew right across the ground straight through the right hoop (I didn't even know it was the right one) and continuing its glorious career hit the King's ball straight into the rose bushes,' there was 'an icy stillness . . . and I realised that never, never was such a thing to happen again.'

Indoors he liked to play bridge or some other card game —bezique may be all right for some, but not for him; or there would be a series of round games in which all could join; or charades; or some dancing—he loved Scottish reels. Practical jokes were very much to his taste, or His Majesty would get into a corner and chuckle over some family scandal narrated in exclamatory whispers by one of the lovelier ladies. No one was allowed to leave the room until the Queen, if she was there, had retired for the night and no man could go to bed until the King gave the lead—he generally sat up until two in the morning or later. It was his habit to count the heads to make sure that this rule was observed, and if anyone was missing then the culprit was sent for, got out of bed, and had to dress and rejoin the company. Poor Sir Dighton Probyn, Keeper of the Privy Purse, who was seventy-five and not at all well, slipped away quietly one night, but was brought back. The King had not the slightest idea who was missing until he saw the sad-eyed General return feebly to the room.

In the morning at eight-thirty, tea was brought to one's bed with some Marie biscuits. For the men, a small brass pitcher of shaving water, for the women a large white enamel jug, also containing hot water, would be placed on the wash-stand beside the attractive china jug of cold water and the enormous bowl in which they had to wash. If a bath was possible before breakfast, they would be informed of this and the water would be turned on by the valet or the maid.

Breakfast was an hour later: one had to go downstairs for it. In the dining-room the guests would arrive in ones and twos and wander to the various tables against the wall where, over small spirit-lamps, stood large silver dishes containing bacon and eggs, chops, and kippers, as well as a great dish of porridge, and pots of tea and coffee and chocolate. On one of the tables the cold fare was spread out— ham, tongue, cold pheasant and grouse, gallantines and ptarmigan. There was also a profusion of fruit—oranges, bananas, grapes, peaches, pears and apples. Selecting what their appetites prompted, they would make their way to the dining table, on which stood numerous racks of toast and plates of rolls. No newspapers were available at breakfast, possibly because they hadn't yet arrived, but chiefly because it was considered anti-social to read at table.

The rest of the morning was devoted to sport—shooting, hunting, fishing, or going for a run in the motor, but one had to dress for this in long sealskin coats, the women's hats were tied down and their faces swathed in veils, for the cars were open cars very like the open carriages, and the roads were very dusty. On Sunday some of the house party went to church in the landau or victoria or on foot; others sat in the library reading the newspapers or a book. One changed for lunch. And so the week-end progressed. On Monday morning all the guests left.

In these vast houses the resident staff of servants numbered more than forty for indoor work, with at least another forty working in the garden, the coach house and the stables. The rosy-cheeked country maids were in caps and aprons, the men in livery. A strict formality was observed below stairs; when they sat down for meals, precedence was given to the Duchess's maid over the Earl's valet. There was a lot of gossip of course, but not in the steward's room if the butler was present.

Away from the house, on their evenings off and while on leave, the servants' meals and their diversions were of course very different. They sat down to a 'high tea' of winkles and bloaters, watercress and pickles, bread and butter, marmalade and cake, with sometimes corned-beef. Their amusements were found in the music hall in the nearest town, which all the famous London artistes visited in turn —George Robey with his heavy arched eyebrows, tiny billy-cock hat and short cane; Harry Lauder singing 'Roamin' in the Gloamin'' and 'Just a Wee Deoch and Doris'; Harry Tate, with his eloquent waxed moustache that kept falling off, doing his celebrated 'Motoring' sketch with a boy who kept calling him 'Papa' (how the King laughed at that); plump little Florrie Forde, who brought tears to every eye as she sang 'The Last Good-bye' during the South African war; Billy Merson singing 'The Spaniard that Blighted My Life' and 'Yacki-Hicki-Doola'; Marie Lloyd with her naughty patter and mildly suggestive songs like 'Every Little Movement Has a Meaning of Its Own' and 'A Little of What You Fancy Does You Good'; Little Tich dancing in his enormous flabby-tipped shoes, almost a yard long—how wonderfully he manipulated them!— and Eugene Stratton, the 'chocolate-coloured coon', whose 'Lily of Laguna' never failed to bring the house down.

In every town, and more so in London, the streets swarmed with house-maids in their neat pink or blue caps and white aprons hurrying with a letter to the slim red pillar box. At every basement window one caught a glimpse of the cook gazing expectantly up the area steps for her helmeted police 'copper' to step down for a cup of tea or a plate of hot soup. Buzzing about behind her would be the 'tweeny', as the 'between-maid' was called, with scruffy dress and hair because her work made it so. And at the windows upstairs the maids would be shaking out the dusters ('Waving to me?' some passer-by usually asked), or beating a rug over the rail of the drawing-room balcony. But this only happened in the best London houses in the summer; for the rest of the year these houses were empty, the windows shuttered, the furniture shrouded, while their owners, having moved to their country residences, went from one country mansion to another for the week-end.

CHAPTER 10

The Women in the King's Life

The main duty of every hostess if the King happened to be staying for the week-end was to seat beside him at lunch and dinner a beautiful woman who was also an entertaining talker, for the King was easily bored: his mouth would droop at the corners and he would drum on the table and say 'Yes, yes . . . quite so.' Ponsonby, his secretary, describing a visit to Lord Howe's house, says: 'About the fourth night I sat next to Lady de Grey, who sat by the King, and she whispered, "For Heaven's sake suggest a topic for me to discuss with the King as I have sat next to him for three nights." I replied, "Give away your relations and friends and repeat any secrets about them." She laughed and said, "But I did that the first night!" '[1]

Margot Asquith, wife of the Liberal Prime Minister, says of the King: 'His early training was of a kind to make him long for a little latitude in pleasure. . . . Like Disraeli, he delighted in the society of women. He was stimulated by their company, intrigued by their entanglements, flattered by their confidence, and valued their counsel, and though the most loyal of friends he was a professional love-maker.'[15]

It would be wrong to assume that the King's only interest in women was to have an *affaire* with them. That he had many *affaires* is indisputable, but there were a great many other women in his life from whom all he sought was a diverting companionship. Margot Asquith was herself one of these. He met her when she was not yet twenty-one. She had just come to London and knew very few people. Her brother Eddy, later Lord Glenconner, took her to Ascot with tickets for the Royal Enclosure. Edward, then Prince of Wales and more than twice her age, came up while she was talking to Lady Dalhousie and asked her to present Margot to him. This done, he talked for a while and then invited Margot to accompany him to the Paddock to see the horses saddled for the next race.

'Walking slowly across the crowded lawn in the grilling sunshine,' she writes, 'I observed everyone making way for us with lifted hats and low curtsies. The Prince appeared to me then—as he did every time I met him—to be the happiest man in the world. . . . He asked me if I was fond of racing. I told him it was the first time I had ever been to a race-meeting, and that I did not know the name of a single trainer, owner, or race-horse. . . . My extreme ignorance delighted him.' He asked her to suggest a horse they could back for the next race. By luck the horse of her choice won. He took her on to lunch with him in the Guards' tent and later 'strolled about among the coaches, costers, gipsies and acrobats'. It was an exciting day for a girl in her first season out. On returning to the Royal Enclosure Margot curtsied and left to look for her brother.

'The next day,' she adds, 'the Prince sent me a gold sharkskin cigarette case with a diamond and sapphire clasp,' but while riding in Rotten Row shortly afterwards to her great distress it fell out of her pocket and was lost. She often met the Prince at lunch, generally in the company of others—'a kinder, more considerate and courteous man never lived'. Later, after her husband became Prime Minister and she saw a great deal of the King, she noted: 'He was a man of wisdom and discretion, who from a rare knowledge of his own limitations seldom attempted anything that he could not accomplish.'

A different and intimate relationship developed between Edward and Lillie Langtry, the most famous of his mistresses.

He first met her in 1877 when he was Prince of Wales: he was thirty-six, she was twenty-four. Three years earlier she had married Edward Langtry, a pudgy, walrus-moustached widower with not very much money though he amused himself with racing yachts and cutters. The marriage was solemnised by Lillie's father, who was Dean of Jersey. Tall, fair-haired, with a skin as translucent as alabaster, and large, captivating grey eyes, her loveliness was a complete departure from the languid, rosebud-mouthed beauties of the time. Her very first appearance in a London drawing-room caused a sensation. Women stood on tiptoe to look at her, and Lord Randolph Churchill was no less impressed than the rest. He wrote to his wife afterwards: 'I took in to dinner a Mrs Langtry, a most beautiful creature, quite unknown, very poor, and they say has only one black dress.' The news of her beauty spread. She was photographed. Picture postcards of her were displayed in every shop window. The artists Millais and Whistler thought her the most beautiful woman they had ever seen, Oscar Wilde sang her praises rapturously, and it was inevitable that before long the Prince of Wales should want to meet her: he came on from a diplomatic reception to a supper party arranged for this purpose and arrived wearing the blue ribbon of the Garter and glittering with decorations.

He found her fascinating and the next morning a note was sent her by hand to say that the Prince of Wales would be pleased to call on her that afternoon. The visit to her modest house in Norfolk Street off Park Lane marked the beginning of an attachment that was to last for some years. He drove about London with her in an open landau. They rode together in Rotten Row before breakfast and sometimes again at seven in the evening. He even took her to Paris for the week-end and to Monte Carlo. Every hostess eager to have the Prince for dinner made sure of it by inviting Lillie Langtry too. All London talked of the new infatuation and soon it was referred to openly in the newspapers of America and France.

Princess Alexandra, saddened in the earlier years of her

marriage by such romantic interludes, had learned to accept the situation and to make allowances. It was said by her closer friends that she idolised her husband: certainly her love for him was understanding and accommodating. Throughout the Mordaunt divorce case she stood loyally by him. On the night the case ended she and the Prince were guests at dinner of Gladstone, the Prime Minister. Gladstone's niece, Lady Frederick Cavendish, records in her diary:[19] 'The dinner and evening went off well; the Princess looked lovely, but *very* sad when she was not exerting herself.'

In time she resigned herself to it: it was the way men in that station behaved. The King of Denmark, whom her father eventually succeeded, had taken morganatically as his third wife a plump milliner whom the family had always regarded as his mistress. She was aware too of what had gone on at the court of Napoleon the Third in Paris, of the numerous mistresses the lovely Empress Eugénie had to bring herself to accept. Rich Frenchmen still took their bejewelled lady friends to the opera as a sort of status symbol, and perhaps also as a display of their virility long after it had waned. It betrayed too their secret yearning for a harem such as the Sultans and Maharajahs possessed—a shrill protest against the puritanism of the Victorian era. It came to its fullest flowering in the Paris Edward so loved and was to be sustained in proud magnificence throughout the Edwardian reign.

In turn, with unwavering devotion towards her, the King was tolerant of her various failings. He found her unpunctuality most irritating.[1] It was something her parents had tried hard to correct during her childhood—as a punishment they would make her stand up at the table while they sat and drank coffee. But she never outgrew it. Whatever the social demands, whatever the importance and urgency of their engagements, she was rarely less than half an hour late. Often the Prince had to wait for close on an hour while eminent visitors and even official deputations cooled their heels in another room. Her Majesty would emerge looking lovely as always but unperturbed. 'Am I late?' she would ask and the King, angry but without a word of reproach, would rise and go with her to join their guests. The clocks at Sandringham were kept half an hour fast (though it was generally believed this was done for daylight saving) and it was not until his grandson King Edward the Eighth came to the throne in 1936 that these clocks were set right.

Queen Alexandra also suffered acutely from deafness. It was an affliction she had inherited from her mother, who was deaf at a very early age. Alexandra was almost stone deaf by the time Edward came to the throne—a severe handicap at a crucial stage of her life. But with her gay, light-hearted, ceaseless chatter she was able to cover up the defect. She talked, Lord Esher tells us,[20] to a dozen people at the same time without hearing a word of what was said. 'She was in excellent spirits and full of rag and mischief,' he states; and again: 'She was in tearing spirits.'

And so with Lillie Langtry, as with his other mistresses, Alexandra put herself out to be amiable and charming. She invited her to dinner parties and receptions at Marlborough House. Lillie was amusing; the other guests, once they had got over their curiosity, found her extremely good company; and of course it made Edward happy to have her there. She went to Cowes (with her husband—he chafed in private but tagged along): they were the guests of the Prince's friend Sir Allen Young in his schooner *Helen*, but were constantly invited to the Royal Yacht, where they dined with a small select company and danced on the illuminated deck. Occasionally she stayed with him aboard the *Osborne*.

A public scandal was only narrowly averted. One afternoon, two years after their first meeting, the streets were full of placards announcing: 'Langtry Divorce Case—Names of Co-respondents.' The paper, *Town Talk*, carried a story that Langtry was citing the Prince of Wales, Lord Lauderdale and others. Lillie's husband immediately brought an action for criminal libel against the editor and Lillie and the Prince went off to Paris together. At the trial the editor pleaded guilty and was sent to prison for eighteen months.

At house parties at week-ends, where Lillie was invariably a guest if the Prince (and sometimes the Princess too) happened to be staying, she joined in the practical jokes and hoaxes which he so enjoyed. They were often quite childish, like making apple-pie beds and putting in beds hot-water bottles that leaked. In time she became daring enough to practise some of these jokes on the Prince. She pretended one night at dinner that the soup was cold. The Prince took a spoonful, found it scalding and burnt his tongue. Another time she tipped some champagne down the back of his collar. While she roared with laughter and the guests looked on embarrassed, the Prince's face became red with anger, and he was not appeased when cartoons of the incident appeared in the American press. It was too much and led to the ending of their more intimate relationship—or perhaps he had already tired of her. But as always his loyalty remained undiminished and he still saw her and tried to help her.

Various members of his circle scrambled for the thread he had dropped, among them his younger brother Leopold, Duke of Albany, and his nephew Prince Louis of Battenberg, who later changed his name to Mountbatten and was the father of Earl Mountbatten of Burma. It was some months after this that Lillie Langtry became pregnant. Princess Alexandra had the first inkling of it during a small dinner party at Marlborough House. She noticed that Lillie Langtry looked unwell, sent her home instantly and asked her doctor to go and see her. The next day she herself called. Lillie tried to get up from the sofa, but Alexandra insisted she should not attempt to rise and poured out tea for her.[54]

The child, a girl, was born abroad, either in Paris or in Biarritz, it is not known definitely where, nor is it certain who the father was. Lillie's closest friends believed Prince Louis was responsible, but it was much more widely assumed that Edward was the actual parent: some wondered at the time if he allowed this impression to prevail in order to protect his nephew or possibly because he felt it flattering to his reputation to be regarded as a Casanova. Lillie herself has said that one night after dinner, Edward jestingly tossed a sovereign to decide who was the father. He lost the toss and as a forfeit gave her a golden statuette of herself in the nude.

It was shortly after the confinement that Edward advised her to go on the stage. He knew of her financial difficulties (Langtry was no longer supporting her and bailiffs were in her house in Norfolk Street), and promised to help her. She took his advice and later in that same year, 1881, made her début at the Haymarket Theatre as Kate Hardcastle in *She Stoops to Conquer*. Both Edward and Alexandra were present on the opening night. Socially it was a fantastic success. A distinguished audience filled the theatre: 'the house overflowed', to use *The Times* phrase, 'with rank, fashion and celebrity'; but otherwise it was a failure. Clement Scott, the outstanding dramatic critic of the day, gave her a devastating critique. 'Mrs Langtry,' he wrote, 'intended us to suppose by this performance to put herself up for hire to the highest managerial figure in the theatrical market and therefore we are justified in strongly and honestly reminding her that without positive genius there is no royal road to eminence, even in the histrionic art; and that a novice must stoop to pick up the rudiments and master them before she can conquer its difficulties. Mrs Langtry is of too solid a physique for any light skittish movement; her laugh not yet being under control appears forced and painful; and her action is as constrained and mechanical as an Eton sixth form boy on speech-day.'

Many of the other reviews were equally damaging, but she was not discouraged. She remained on the stage for many years, went on numerous tours in the provinces and to America and South Africa; she also took on a succession of lovers: the most distinguished of them was the Crown Prince Rudolf of Austria, who, when chided by her at a ball for not wearing gloves on that warm night to protect her lovely pink dress of clinging *crêpe de chine*, replied 'It is you who are sweating, Madame': not many years later he committed suicide with his mistress at Mayerling.

Margot Asquith saw Lillie Langtry involved in an unusual scene in Hyde Park and has left this vivid record of it: 'One day, when I was riding, I saw Mrs Langtry—who was accompanied by Lord Lonsdale—pause at the railings in Rotten Row to talk to a man of her acquaintance. I do not know what she could have said to him, but after a brief exchange of words, Lord Lonsdale jumped off his horse, sprang over the railings, and with clenched fists hit Mrs Langtry's admirer in the face. Upon this, a free fight ensued, and to the delight of the surprised spectators, Lord Lonsdale knocked his adversary down. . . . It caused an uproar in London, and for many weeks no other subject was discussed.'[15]

Lillie tried to get a divorce from Langtry but he refused to grant it. A year or so before Edward's accession to the throne Langtry was found badly injured at Chester station. He was said to have fallen in front of a railway train; others believed that he had tried to commit suicide. Penniless by now and often drunk, he was taken to Chester lunatic asylum where he died a few days later. Shortly afterwards Lillie Langtry married Hugo de Bathe, who was twenty-six and she nearly twenty years older. They were not much together. In time he inherited his father's baronetcy and Lillie Langtry at last got the title for which she had yearned. She died in 1929 at the age of seventy-five.

An early successor to Lillie Langtry in Edward's affections was the Countess of Warwick—at that time Lady Brooke, as her husband had not yet succeeded to the earldom. The grand-daughter of Viscount Maynard and co-heir to that title, she married Brooke in 1881, the year the intimate relationship between Edward and Lillie Langtry came to an end. She was twenty at the time. By birth, by marriage and by her own striking beauty she was drawn into the Marlborough House set—'it was a bit of idle pleasure,' she said afterwards; 'in London, during the season, the special achievement of the Marlborough House set was to turn night into day. We would dine late and long, trifle with the Opera for an hour or so, or watch the Ballet at the Empire, then go on to as many houses as we could crowd in.'[55] Under Edward's influence, she says, a great stimulus was given to music, though his own taste was of the simplest. 'He was himself intolerant of classical music with certain exceptions, and any effort by Sir Walter Parratt, the Master of the King's Musick, to introduce it into programmes for him was disastrous: its only effect was to bring the concert to an untimely end.' He liked Wagner, loved going to the opera and delighted in a performance by Sousa and his band.

Edward often visited Lady Warwick at her house at Easton in Essex—a magnificent country seat where she dined off gold plate and entertained the elect. A crowd would gather at the railway station to see him arrive for the weekend and he would drive off in a wagonette, courteously responsive to their greetings, but he did wish he could enjoy some privacy sometimes: it was his strict rule in every club he joined that he should not be recognised.

It was towards the end of the eighties that the friendship with Lady Warwick became more intimate. As with Lillie Langtry he took her to Paris. They did the round of the theatres, dined and supped at the famous restaurants, went shopping and visited some of the art galleries. On one of these visits he took her to the top of the Eiffel Tower, erected for the Paris Exhibition of 1889 to mark the centenary of the French Revolution. Together they climbed the outside staircase to the foot of the flagstaff and gazed at the delightful panorama of the Seine with its islands and many bridges and the vast spreading city around. Sometimes Lady Warwick was accompanied by her sister or they were joined later by Lord Warwick.

King Edward, she records in her memoirs, was 'an intimate and dear friend for many years. . . . What a man or woman might do in private,' she goes on, 'was their own affair, but our rule was No Scandal! Whenever there was a threat of impending trouble, pressure would be brought to bear, sometimes from the highest quarters, and almost always successfully. We realised that publicity would cause

Lillie Langtry

Prince Edward and Princess Alexandra (seated centre) with their suite in Egypt 1869

Below Prince Edward was very fond of dancing

Top Prince Edward leading in Persimmon after winning the Derby in 1896. From a contemporary drawing

Bottom King Edward shooting at Sandringham

Prince Edward at a fancy dress ball at Devonshire House, 1897. He is dressed as the Grand Prior of the order of St John of Jerusalem

Princess Victoria and Princess Maud paddling. Photographed by their mother, Princess Alexandra

Opposite A house party at Windsor Castle, 1907. From left to right: Queen Ena of Spain, King Edward the Seventh, the Empress of Germany, Kaiser Wilhelm the Second, Queen Alexandra, the Queen of Portugal, King Alfonso of Spain, Queen Maud of Norway

Discussing the *Entente Cordiale*. King Edward and President Loubet of France. From a contemporary drawing

chattering tongues, and as we had no intention of changing our mode of living, we saw to it that five out of every six scandals never reached the outside world.' At the time of the Jameson raid which preceded the South African war, the Kaiser's telegram to Kruger so angered her that she was said to have sent a stern letter of protest to him. There was no truth in this, but the German Ambassador in Paris, Count Münster, hearing of it, wrote to Lady Warwick's mother. The letter, he said, was 'most impertinent. She ought to have dressed in black and held her tongue and her pen.' Edward was furious. He drafted a letter for Lady Warwick to send to Münster. 'Mamma (or my mother),' the draft began, 'has shown me your letter. . . . Lady War-wick has not the honour of His Majesty's acquaintance and it was not therefore likely she should write to him. . . . Count Münster should have disbelieved so palpable a lie! This is, however, not the first time you have said unkind things about me to Mamma, as a few years ago you asked her at Homburg when I was going to be divorced!' Lady Warwick copied out the letter and sent it. The Count did not answer.

In the nineties politics began to engage Lady Warwick's interest. She aired some of her views to Edward: they were not at all to his taste, and in any case he did not like women to enter that arena. Lady Warwick's politics moreover went too far in his view. Liberalism was all right, he believed in progress, but she joined the Socialist party in 1895, and, although his unwavering loyalty sustained their friendship (he continued to visit her at Easton and planted many trees there), the closeness of the relationship came to an end.

The Prince's eye had already alighted on Mrs Luke Wheeler, who was regarded by many as even lovelier than Lillie Langtry. He called on her and invited her to come for a drive with him in his brougham. She refused. He told her not to mind what people might say, they were already saying all sorts of things about him and he didn't mind at all. 'Perhaps not, Sir,' she replied, 'but so far they say nothing about me, and I don't mean that they should.'[7]

A year or so later a close, and intimate friendship was established with Mrs Alice Keppel, the wife of George Keppel, a younger son of the Earl of Albemarle. She too was very lovely, with large turquoise eyes, a very fair skin and light chestnut hair. Her figure was slender, but her bosom was well developed; she thus had a natural hour-glass shape, without the aid of pads. Their meeting occurred by chance. Sir John Leslie, Winston Churchill's Uncle Jack, was walking at Sandown Races with Mrs Keppel, then still in her twenties, when the Prince of Wales came by. He stopped and Mrs Keppel was introduced. 'The Prince immediately asked her to accompany him and his face lit up with such a smile,' Sir John's wife said later,[9] 'and Jacksy knew he would not see her again for a long time!' Alice Keppel was lively, amusing, witty, intelligent and above all discreet: she was the last of the many beautiful women in Edward's life and their association, which began in the late nineties, endured to the end of his reign. She had a way of restoring his good humour even when he was thoroughly put out.

One evening, shortly after his accession, he was engaged in a game of bridge with Mrs Keppel as his partner. He had a succession of bad hands and kept grumbling about them. Mrs Keppel, to force the play into their opponents' camp, bid 'No trumps' but was left to play it out. Edward as dummy put his cards down: there was hardly a trick in it. Mrs Keppel glanced at her hand again and sighed. Then looking at Edward, she observed: 'All I can say, Sire, is "God Save the King and preserve Mrs Keppel!"' He roared with laughter. His mood passed.

She and her husband, who was in the Army, lived in a narrow, high house in Portman Square. They had not a great deal of money. There was one daughter, Violet, and some years later in 1900, a second daughter arrived. The younger child, Sonia, remembers the King well, for he often went round to their house. She recalls his 'kind, deep voice' and his 'plump, be-ringed hands' and of course also his cigars. To her he was 'Kingy'. Sometimes, she says,[56] he 'came to tea with Mamma, and was there when I appeared at six o'clock. On such occasions he and I devised a fascinating game. With a fine disregard for the good condition of his trouser, he would lend me his leg, on which I used to start two bits of bread and butter (butter side down), side by side. Then, bets of a penny each were made (my bet provided by Mamma) and the winning piece of bread and butter, depended, of course, on which was the more buttery. The excitement was intense while the contest was on. Sometimes he won, sometimes I did. Although the owner of a Derby winner, Kingy's enthusiasm seemed delightfully unaffected by the quality of his bets.'

Every year for Easter Alice Keppel joined the King at Biarritz, taking her children with her. They stayed at the Villa Eugénie, which was rented yearly by Sir Ernest Cassel, whose daughter and her two children, Edwina and Mary, were also there. The long journey out by train has been described by Alice Keppel's young daughter Sonia. Having normally seen her mother only at stipulated times of the day, it was a shock to discover how her mother prepared herself for a night's sleep in the *wagon lit* they shared. 'Throughout her life,' she writes, 'Mamma wore her beauty without vanity, as she would an old mackintosh. Now, aesthetically, acutely I minded the way she obliterated it for the night. Out of a square, silk case she brought a small pillow, a shapeless nightgown and a mob-cap. Under the nightgown she subdued her beautifully curved body. And, under the cap, she piled her shining, chestnut hair. Next, she greased her face. Then, she helped me up the ladder to my upper berth and kissed me "goodnight". Lastly, she took a strong sleeping-pill, put on black night-spectacles, and lay for dead till morning. I dared not move, and any inclination to go to the lavatory had to be controlled until daylight filtered through the shuttered window. And, even then, I was terrified I would fall down the ladder and wake Mamma.'

They often went on a picnic with the King while in Biarritz. Kingy liked impromptu parties, made up generally of many friends. They set out in motor-cars, which by now were becoming much more reliable, and always the King's car went in front. The last car carried the picnic hampers and two footmen. Coming upon what he regarded as a suitable site, he gave the signal to stop. The cars pulled up. The footmen leapt out. Chairs were produced, tables were set up and covered with linen table-cloths. Plates and glasses were provided as well as silver dishes. There was every variety of cold food and iced-cup in silver-plated containers. But for some reason, she adds, 'Kingy had a preference for picnicking by the side of the road. On Easter Day, inevitably, this was packed with carriages and the first motor-cars, all covered with dust, and when we parked by the roadside, most of the traffic parked with us. Much of Kingy's enjoyment of these picnics was based on his supposed anonymity and, delightedly, he would respond to an assumed name in his deep, unmistakable voice, unaware that most of the crowd was playing up to him.' The King's accent in fact was gutturally Germanic. The 'g' was hard and came from the depth of his throat; the 'r' was thick and reverberative: he said 'ar-r-rangement'. It was much more marked in his speech than in that of his brothers.

After a three weeks' stay the journey home was begun. It was generally broken in Paris where Alice Keppel did some shopping. She bought gloves and shoes from the Nain Bleu in the Rue St Honoré and visited Worth, her dressmaker, while the children whirled about on the merry-go-rounds on the Champs-Elysées with Nannie.

In 1905 a comment by the Kaiser about Edward's behaviour caused the King intense annoyance. A letter from Count Metternich, the German Ambassador in London, to Prince von Bülow, the German Chancellor, stated: 'King Edward's displeasure with His Majesty can be attributed to more than politics. . . . It is said that the Emperor talked freely in yachting circles about the "looseness" of English Society, and in particular about King Edward's relationship with Mrs Keppel. King Edward is very touchy on this subject and this seems to have annoyed him especially.'[57]

Of course Queen Alexandra knew all about it and, as with the others, she constantly invited Mrs Keppel to dinner and receptions at the Palace and to stay at Sandringham and Windsor; because she saw that Edward was always in a good humour in her company, she did everything she could to assist and so Mrs Keppel was often and openly spoken of as His Majesty's second wife. Margot Asquith lays emphasis on Alice Keppel's happy personality and adds: 'She is a plucky woman of fashion; human, adventurous, and gay, who in spite of doing what she liked all her life, has never made an enemy.' When, after being at No. 10 Downing Street for nine years, the Asquiths had to leave, they found themselves with nowhere to stay and Alice Keppel, always large-hearted and kind, gave up her own bedroom and sitting-room for them to live in for as many months as they liked.

Of the many lovely women in King Edward's life the great majority were just friends—women like Lady Randolph Churchill, Lady de Grey (who eventually became the Marchioness of Ripon), Mrs Cornwallis-West and her equally beautiful daughter Daisy, who married the Prince of Pless—her brother George Cornwallis-West later married Lady Randolph Churchill, who was many years his senior. Daisy gives a very revealing picture of a week-end house party in 1909 at which the King was present. It was at Eaton, the home of her sister Shelagh, who was married to the Duke of Westminster, and provides, as she says, 'an example of King Edward's warm nature, kindly heart and simple homeliness'.

'I was sitting next to him at luncheon one day,' she writes,[50] 'when he asked: "What are you doing this afternoon?"

' "Oh, nothing very amusing, Sir; motoring over to see my Granny* at Brynedwyn: it is not far from here." '

To her surprise he said, 'I will come as well.' She was wondering what on earth she would do with the King in Granny's little cottage. She indicated that there would

* Lady Olivia Fitzpatrick, who was then in her eighty-sixth year.

85

not be much room in the car as Mrs Keppel was coming too, but the King was not to be put off.

'When we arrived,' she goes on, 'I hurried ahead to prepare Granny a bit. She had just come in from a drive. Her bonnet was crooked, her lovely white hair all blown about and her nose red. The idea of seeing the King did not at all amuse her. She asked why he had come as she had nothing particular to show him. However the King was delightful, though he started badly by sitting down in Granny's favourite chair. He made outrageous love to the old lady and in a few minutes they were both flirting desperately. Granny could never resist flirting and neither could the King. . . .

'The King said: "Is it true that my Mother sent you away from Court for trying to flirt with my father?"

' "I can't quite remember, Sir; most likely I wanted to flirt with your father: he was a very good-looking man. . . ." We had tea and a delightfully cosy afternoon.'

Gaiety and frivolity mingled with elegance and stateliness in the life of Edward and Alexandra from the very outset of their marriage and set the tone that became the distinctive mark of the Edwardian era. Their more liberal ideas both on social eligibility and behaviour were widely adopted. Professional beauties came into their own and it was possible for Rosa Lewis and the Cavendish Hotel in Jermyn Street to flourish. It was the Cavendish before Rosa took it over in 1902, a private hotel of the highest class with a number of very respectable permanent residents. Lord Avon's father, Sir William Eden, for example, had a suite of rooms there, so did Lord Ribblesdale, and occasionally Lord Roberts and Lord Kitchener stayed there too: others came to dine either alone or with a group of friends. Rosa enlarged the place by taking over the adjoining houses and it became possible to enter it secretly through the stable-yard at the back, thus providing a comfortable alternative to the private supper rooms to which one took an actress after the theatre; and there were a number of unattached girls about, some of them well-bred though not well-off. Most famous of the rooms at that time was one upstairs known as the 'Elinor Glyn Room', because Lord Curzon often brought that lovely author to dine there.

King Edward's dual life was well known and accepted—the outward ceremonial life as monarch, seen with the panoply of State as at the opening of Parliament, the Trooping the Colour, the elegant evening receptions and levées, and his life as a man of pleasure with beautiful women as his companions. But there was in fact a third life of which the world knew nothing because the King insisted on keep-it private, and that was his personal, intimate life with the Queen. The strictest privacy was maintained in Buckingham Palace where Their Majesties kept to their own apartments whenever it was possible to draw away from the social and official rounds. To some extent this was observed at Windsor Castle as well, but with guests in residence there, since it was a country rather than a town home, it was inescapable that they should mingle with their guests in the evening. But it should not be overlooked that his devotion to the Queen was greater than his varied and often irregular mode of life would suggest.

It used to be said maliciously that the high collar of pearls or diamonds was worn by Queen Alexandra to hide a scar on her throat, self-inflicted in a moment of acute unhappiness over her husband's love-affairs. Nothing could be further from the truth. In fact the first of her jewelled high collars, which was made of pearls, was given to Alexandra as a wedding present by the King of Denmark. She later had one made of diamonds. Fashion decreed that the neck should be entirely encased in a collar of lace which reached almost to the tips of the ears and not only Queen Alexandra but all women in society wore high-collared dresses: it was the counterpart of the high stiff collars worn by men at the time. Queen Alexandra had in fact an extremely happy disposition. Edward showered her with gifts and her letters to Queen Victoria as well as to her friends were strewn with evidence of her deep devotion to him.

CHAPTER 11

The Postponed Coronation

To the populace the highlight of the new reign was to be the Coronation. There had not been a Coronation for sixty-four years, and this was to provide the pageantry and jubilation of which they had been cheated at the time of Edward's marriage forty years ago. Its date had been selected by the King: he placed it eighteen months ahead in the hope that the South African war would be over by then—and in fact the hope was fulfilled with the slight margin of only a few days to spare.

The King, being a great lover of ceremony, personally supervised all the arrangements. An important change from the normal procedure was introduced by him: he insisted that all crowned heads and reigning princes should be excluded and only their heirs should be invited. The reason for this, he explained in a letter to the Foreign Secretary, Lord Lansdowne, was 'the extreme difficulty of precedence'. But difficulties nevertheless arose. In order that the Kaiser should not take offence, the Crown Prince of Germany, who became the jibe of cartoonists as 'Little Willie' during the First World War, was to have precedence over the heirs-apparent of Russia, Austria and Italy; but even so the Kaiser refused to accept the invitation. He declared there had been rumours of his son's frivolous behaviour during a previous visit to England and he felt it would be better if the young man stayed away and continued his studies. The rumours were in fact based on actual reports sent to the Kaiser by Count Eulenburg, the Crown Prince's escort. The young Prince had got involved in a number of love affairs and was found in bed with a lady at one of the country houses where he was a guest.[25] The Kaiser, the only European sovereign not to accept the invitation, sent his younger brother Prince Henry of Prussia instead. Austria was represented by the Archduke Franz Ferdinand, whose murder on 28th June 1914 led to the outbreak of the First World War.

In the second week of June 1902 the guests began to arrive. They came from Russia and Spain, the United States and Japan, Siam and China, Zanzibar, Egypt and Abyssinia, each with a dozen attendants. The trains poured into London and the amount of luggage they brought was stupendous. Banquets and receptions had been arranged for them, but suddenly the whisper got round that the King was ill. Not much was said officially beyond the fact that His Majesty had caught a chill while attending a military tattoo at Aldershot in the pouring rain. His doctor Sir Francis Laking was sent for and arrived at a quarter to five in the morning. He 'recognised the presence of an abdominal trouble that might be serious and telegraphed for Sir Thomas Barlow'.* A day later, on Monday, 16th June, he left Aldershot for Windsor, but the Queen stayed to take the review of 30,000 troops in his absence. Ascot week followed and the Queen attended the races alone, much to His Majesty's distress. But he thought it prudent to accept his doctors' advice and stay in bed so that he should be fit for his Coronation in the following week.

On Wednesday, the 18th, his surgeon Sir Frederick Treves found that his temperature had risen and there were symptoms of perityphlitis, but by the week-end the temperature had fallen and the ominous symptoms had disappeared. It was thought that the King was on the road to recovery and would be able after all to go through the arduous

* *The Lancet*, 27th June 1902.

Coronation ceremony. On Monday, 23rd June, with the Coronation only three days off, His Majesty insisted on travelling up to London. His doctors advised him to travel by road, but the official arrangements required him to go by train, and he kept to that. At Paddington station an open carriage and a cavalry escort awaited him and he drove past cheering crowds to Buckingham Palace. To the public it was proof that they need no longer attach any credence to the many alarming rumours. Some, however, thought that he looked pale and very far from well. A question about his health was asked that afternoon in the House of Lords. The Prime Minister, Lord Salisbury, replying with emotion, gave a gloomy and by no means reassuring answer. That night the King did not appear at the State banquet at the Palace nor at the reception that followed. The next morning, while the Coronation rehearsal was in progress at the Abbey, the country and the distinguished visitors learned with dismay that the Coronation would have to be indefinitely postponed. He had been examined that morning by five doctors, who decided unanimously that an immediate operation was essential. But His Majesty refused to agree to it, although he was suffering the acutest pain. 'I must keep faith with my people,' he insisted. 'I must go to the Abbey.' No argument would budge him. 'Then, Sir, you will go in your coffin,' said Sir Frederick Treves finally, pointing out that to delay and face the long and trying ceremony at the Abbey would prove fatal. At that time appendicitis was little known and the word had hardly been used even in medical circles. The operation therefore was not as commonplace or as simple as it has since become, and even the surgeons were fearful of its results.

Shortly after noon that day the operation was performed by Treves at Buckingham Palace. Dr Frederick Hewitt, who gave the anaesthetic, saw the stout, elderly King suddenly turn purple in the face. He said afterwards that, with great presence of mind, he quickly seized the King's beard and jerked his head sharply forward. The King began to breathe again. Treves made an incision and drained the abscess. The appendix was not removed. In the official bulletin the King was still said to have been suffering from 'perityphlitis'.[60] On emerging from the anaesthetic his first words were to ask for his son, later George the Fifth; he also said: 'Will my people ever forgive me?'

Stands, painted a bright scarlet, had been built along the route for seating the public. Flags of the visiting nations were flying from all the public buildings. Banners and bunting, gaily coloured coats-of-arms and enormous crystal constellations for illumination hung above the Mall and along the processional route from the Palace to the Abbey. 'Indefinitely postponed'—that meant all would have to be taken down, the stands would have to be dismantled, the assembled heirs to various thrones and their suites would have to pack their trunks and depart, their journey disappointingly fruitless. The visiting royalties in fact began to leave at once. But they were not the only ones who had come to London for the Coronation. 'The pavements seethed with unaccustomed faces,' said *The Times*,* 'and passage to and fro far from easy upon them.' There was 'an endless flood of vehicles of every kind. There were private carriages, many of them Royal and containing the King's guests, omnibuses, chars-à-bancs, country-carts fitted with longitudinal planks for seats, spring carts, vans, costermongers' carts—and all were loaded, to say nothing of many that were overloaded.'

Then there was the food ordered by Buckingham Palace for the entertainment of the Royal guests—2,500 quails, hundreds of chickens, partridges and sturgeons, fruit, sweets, dessert. A lot of it was sent to the Little Sisters of the Poor and other charities and so reached many poor families living in London's East End.[61] The losses on the stands erected were partly covered by insurance, but they were nevertheless great—St George's Hospital, for example, had spent £2,000 on the erection of stands and had contracted for £500 worth of refreshments. The restaurants too suffered losses: Gunters had a contract for 6,000 guests for the Royal Garden Party and for 1,000 luncheons at the House of Lords.

* 26th June 1902.

Florists and flower-growers all over the country were also seriously affected.

To commemorate the Coronation the King had founded a new order, the Order of Merit, to be conferred by the Sovereign alone for distinction in science, art, literature and the armed services. As he was traditionally regarded as 'the sole fountain of honour', this was to restore in a measure the Sovereign's ancient privilege. The number of its Members was limited to twenty-four, but to begin with only twelve names were announced. They included Lord Roberts, Lord Kitchener, John Morley for literature and G. F. Watts for art. Sir Francis Knollys, the King's secretary, was made a peer. The general honours list was extensive— more than three times the normal length: it bore 1,540 names as against the usual 400 or so.

In the middle of July the King went on board the Royal yacht *Victoria and Albert* to convalesce. He was taken to the train on a stretcher and at Portsmouth blue-jackets carried him to the yacht. The vessel did not leave the Solent. 'You can't think,' he told his assistant secretary Ponsonby, 'what a pleasure it is to get out of my sick-room at Buckingham Palace.' His Majesty had an abhorrence of illness.

He kept to his deck-cabin and the Queen, who 'was in great form and full of jokes,' did all the entertaining. The convalescence was rapid and by the end of July a new date was announced for the Coronation—9th August, seven weeks after the original date. Almost all the distinguished visitors had left by now and the King decided not to invite them to return, but to have only members of his own family drawn from the lesser ruling Princes of Europe. Even so it was not the anticlimax this would suggest, but far surpassed Queen Victoria's Coronation in pomp and magnificence. From all parts of the Empire were drawn units of their armed forces —Sikhs from the Viceroy of India's Bodyguard, wild long-haired men of the Baluchistan Regiment, soldiers from West Africa, Jamaica, the Barbadoes, Dyaks from Borneo, Maoris from New Zealand. From Europe came King Edward's Russian Regiment of Guards, the Danish Regiment of

Hussars, the Austrian Regiment of Hussars and the German Regiment of Dragoon Guards. There was also a magnificently impressive array of Indian Princes in their State uniforms and turbans. The streets were abundantly decorated and at night there were illuminations.

The King's doctors insisted that the service at the Abbey should be abbreviated and the King eventually agreed to this, but he would not hear of ramps being constructed so that he should be wheeled in to avoid climbing steps.

While the royal coach and the Sovereign's escort of Horse Guards waited for him to set out from the Palace, His Majesty, in high spirits, went in his Coronation robes to see his grandchildren, the eldest, David, later the Duke of Windsor, just eight years old. The King performed a few steps of an improvised dance for their diversion. 'There's a funny old grand-papa!' he laughed. Then gaily he set forth.

The service was conducted by the aged Archbishop of Canterbury, Dr Temple, who was in his eighties and very feeble. After placing the crown on the King's head, the Archbishop got down on his knees to pay homage, but found it difficult to get up again. His Majesty, seeing that he was about to fall, leaned forward, clasped him in his arms, and helped him up. Again, while anointing Queen Alexandra, the Archbishop's unsteady hand caused the oil to spill and trickle down Her Majesty's nose.

The King sighed with relief when it was over. He was not tired, he said, but he had received so many telegrams and letters beforehand, prophesying the most dire happenings during the ceremony, that it was a comfort to have come through it all so well.[26] But it was not all over yet. He had further trying ceremonies to face: the investiture of 1,800 Colonial troops, then the investiture of the Indian contingent, and finally the Naval Review at Spithead, for which he went down to Cowes with the Queen. He invited the defeated Boer generals to the Review, feeling it was time to offer them the hand of friendship, but they refused to come. They accepted, however, a personal invitation to a private reception on board his yacht. As their steam launch approached, the Queen, seeing them dressed in black frock-coats, black trousers, black gloves and top-hats, thought they were undertakers. Entertaining them was an inspiration. By his thoughtfulness and tact His Majesty helped to establish a better understanding between the two countries which proved of the utmost advantage in the years ahead and culminated in the establishing of the Union of South Africa during his lifetime.

The visit of the Shah of Persia to the yacht on the next day had not such happy results. Lord Lansdowne, the Foreign Secretary, had unfortunately been of the impression that the King was to confer the Garter on the Shah and the the British Minister in Teheran had already informed the Shah of this. But the King held rigidly to the view that the Garter, because it bore the Cross of St George, should be reserved exclusively for Christian sovereigns and could not be given to infidels, although Queen Victoria had made exceptions in the case of two Sultans of Turkey and had also given it to the Shah's father.

Lansdowne designed a star to replace the Cross and when the Foreign Office despatch box arrived with the design the King was furious. 'He was so angry,' Sir Frederick Ponsonby tells us, 'that he flung the design across the cabin and it went through the porthole and, as I thought, into the sea. Later, however, I found that it had fallen into a steam pinnace and had been brought back by the stoker.'[1] His Majesty sent an extremely angry letter to Lansdowne and refused absolutely to comply with his request. Lansdowne offered his resignation to the Prime Minister, by now A. J. Balfour, and they both went to see the King. After a long and wearying discussion the King said he would think it over. Presently the Shah arrived on board with an enormous suite of attendants. There was not enough room for all of them in the dining saloon and a quarrel began just before lunch. They were told that half of them would get nothing to eat unless they went to the *Osborne* where a meal had been set out for them. Eventually, rather reluctantly, they agreed.

The King tried to persuade the Shah to accept the Order

of the Bath and offered a bust of himself as well, but the Shah refused flatly and left the yacht in a bad temper. Some months later the King finally gave him the Garter.

It had after all been a great Season in London despite the postponement. Entertaining was on an unprecedented scale. The large town houses—Dorchester House and Londonderry House in Park Lane, Lansdowne House in Berkeley Square, Devonshire House in Piccadilly, and many others—were still residences: there were in fact hardly any flats in the West End and not many hotels. Night after night at one or other of these houses there were balls and receptions. Crowds gathered at the gates to see the guests arrive, much as they were to do in later years outside the big cinemas to see film stars. Eagerly heads were craned to catch a glimpse of the elegantly dressed tiara-ed ladies in the carriages drawn by proud, handsome horses, with a liveried coachman on the box and a liveried footman to help them alight. Few of the guests were recognised: their photographs rarely appeared in the ha'penny morning and evening newspapers. But their dresses and jewels drew gasps and there were coo's of delight as the bachelors drove up in the gondolas of London, the hansom cabs, many of which were privately owned. No one arrived by motor. Although it was five years since the King had bought his Daimler and cars were no longer preceded by a man with a red flag, the motor-car, still an open, roofless vehicle, was not yet either reliable or elegant, nor would it have been kind to the wonderful coiffures and feathered adornments of the ladies. Cars were used, as the King used his, chiefly for jaunts into the country.

At these receptions in the great houses there was always an orchestra and famous singers like Melba and pianists like Paderewski were hired to entertain the guests. At Lady (Arthur) Paget's Mary Garden sang and Jeanne Granier recited: Lady Warwick was there and so was Mrs Keppel as well as the Duke and Duchess of Westminster: before the end of the reign, that is to say within eight years, part of the evening's entertainment was provided by the

95

bioscope, with the audience seated in the dark laughing their heads off at a new Mack Sennett silent film, but not yet at Charlie Chaplin—he came four years later. A professional dancer would give a display of the Negro dance, the cake walk, but the guests would not dream of dancing it: when the floor was cleared, after the entertainers had left, the band struck up a waltz or the lancers in the vast ballroom.

CHAPTER 12

The King's Extensive Travels

Throughout the long Victorian era alliance by marriage seemed to be regarded as a more powerful and enduring bond between nations than alliance by treaty. Queen Victoria had a large number of sons and daughters and their marriages provided important and effective links with the crowned heads of Europe who at that time were often the actual rulers. No such link could of course be established with the two great republics of France and the United States of America whose rulers were selected by ballot rather than by birth.

As a result of these marriages King Edward VII was the uncle of Kaiser Wilhem II through the marriage of Queen Victoria's eldest daughter, also named Victoria, with the heir to the German throne, who later became the Emperor Frederick: their daughter Sophia married King Constantine of Greece, who in consequence was another nephew of Edward's.

Through his own marriage to Princess Alexandra of Denmark, Edward was the son-in-law of one King of Denmark and the brother-in-law of another: their daughter Maud married King Haakon VII of Norway.

Edward's sister Alice was the mother of Alix, Tsaritsa of Russia by her marriage to Nicholas II, the last Tsar of Russia. Edward's brother Alfred, Duke of Edinburgh and

Saxe-Coburg-Gotha, married a daughter of the Tsar of Russia: one of their daughters became Queen of Rumania.

Edward's brother Arthur, Duke of Connaught, married a Prussian Princess, their daughter became Queen of Sweden.

His sister Beatrice was the mother of the Queen of Spain, whose husband Alfonso XIII was the last King of that country.

Edward was thus the uncle of the rulers of Germany Russia, Greece, Rumania and Sweden, father-in-law of the King of Norway and brother-in-law of the King of Denmark. Some of these links were further strengthened by various marriages of Queen Alexandra's family: for example, Alexandra's sister Dagmar was the mother of Tsar Nicholas II of Russia, who in turn was married to Edward's niece; King Edward was thus doubly the uncle of the Tsar: Alexandra's brother was King George I of Greece, which again doubled Edward's link with Greece. Far more extensive still were the links established by the marriage of cousins: these forged close alliances with Belgium (whose first King was Queen Victoria's Uncle Leopold), with Austria, Hanover and the rulers of an assorted number of German principalities.

To visit his relatives involved a great deal of travelling, which fortunately he loved. But his journeys were not confined to visiting relatives. He began his trips abroad at the early age of thirteen when he went to Paris with his parents. It was his first glimpse of the gay city he later learned to adore. Queen Victoria was on a State visit to the Emperor Napoleon the Third: she had also taken her daughter Victoria. Dressed in the Stuart kilt, Edward captivated all hearts with his charming manners and his prettily spoken French. With the Queen he went to the tomb of Napoleon Bonaparte in the Invalides, and she made him get down on his knees to pay homage to Britain's great enemy. On their last night he asked the Empress if he and his sister could stay for a day or two longer. The Empress replied that the Queen would not like to be parted from them.

'Don't think that,' the Prince said. 'We have eight children at home and they can get on quite well without us.'[4]

On one of his university vacations, he was sent to Rome for three months under the care of a military Governor: the purpose of the trip was that he should study archaeology and art—he was not yet seventeen. Two years later he went to Germany for Easter to visit relatives. He dined with the Queen's uncle Leopold in Brussels, spent a day with his sister Vicky who was by now married to the Crown Prince of Germany and went to Coburg and Gotha to see his father's brother and to call on Stockmar, with somewhat mixed feelings since Stockmar was the real architect of his cruelly strict upbringing. There was some criticism of his behaviour later when the news got back that he had tried to kiss a pretty girl.

In the summer of that same year, 1860, when he was still eighteen, he left for Canada and the United States of America. Even this was to form a part of his education. Tutors accompanied him, the supervision of a Governor remained, speeches written for him by his father had to be studied on the voyage out, and the rigid routine drawn up for the tour had to be strictly observed. In Canada he was to perform his first public duties as Prince of Wales. To this visit the Queen had been committed by an impulsive promise made some years before when, in return for the contingent sent by Canada to the Crimean War, she declared that her son would visit the Dominion. He went on to America at the request of the President of the United States, but the Queen would not hear of his going as Prince of Wales and Heir to the Throne, so he travelled *incognito*, using the least exalted of his titles—Baron Renfrew; he was to be the President's private guest and the intention was that the Prince should study 'the social and economic conditions' in that country.[2]

It turned out otherwise. Despite the attempted concealment of his identity, the Prince was besieged by wildly excited admirers. At a ball in New York to which 4,000 guests had been invited, more than 5,000 managed to break in, the floor collapsed and dancing had to wait for nearly two hours while a horde of carpenters were busily engaged on its repair. Members of that great republic which had thrown off the British yoke less than a hundred years before and had spat at the very mention of the name of King George the Third, now struggled frenziedly to secure the bones left on his plate by that King's great-grandson, fought eagerly for the cigar-ends he threw away and even for the water in which he washed.[3] It was the year of the critical election which led to Lincoln becoming President. 'Come back in four years and run for President!' a man in the crowd yelled as the Prince was setting out on his long, exhausting, twenty-six-day voyage home.

General Bruce, his Governor, reported to the anxious parents that the Prince had acquired 'a regrettable notion of his own importance'. It was precisely what Prince Albert had feared would happen. He decided that the Prince would have to be told that the adulation was given to the Queen's representative and was not a personal tribute to him. The feelings of Prince Albert must have suffered a pang as he realised that his own public appearances on behalf of the Queen and even his painstaking speeches were received by the loyal people of Britain with no more than cool respect. To be fêted and spoiled at the immature age of eighteen, to be fawned on by lovely young women vying for his smile—was it any wonder the boy's head had been turned. Discipline would have to be tightened. His studies had been unnecessarily interrupted for four months. That lost time would somehow have to be made up. What angered Prince Albert still further was a cartoon in *Punch* depicting Prince Edward as a dissolute young man in an armchair, his feet on the fender, his top-hat tipped over his brow, a glass in his hand and a cigar stuck into the corner of his mouth, saying to his father: 'Now, Sir-ree, if you'll sit down and liquor up I'll tell you all about my travels.'

His military training at the Curragh in Ireland took place in the succeeding summer and was followed, as we have seen, by the death of his father.

At the Queen's wish, as she could not bear to have him near her, he set out on his next journey almost immediately. It took him to the Near East. He travelled through Germany to Austria, then to Egypt, Palestine and Syria and was away for more than five months. On his way home he called at Constantinople and Athens.

He found his stay in Egypt most enjoyable. The country was then under Turkish rule and the Viceroy was lavish in his hospitality. He was given a palace to live in, and in high spirits he rode a donkey through the streets of Cairo to the astonishment and horror of an elderly Pasha who was in attendance,[5] travelled up the Nile as far as Aswan, stopping to look at the old temples on the way (in the ruins of the temple of Karnac at Luxor his companion Dean Stanley held a service), shot crocodiles, and spent his idle time on board reading among other books *East Lynne* by Mrs Humphrey Ward, which roused him to the utmost enthusiasm.

After his marriage in the following year Edward often went to Denmark. He made his first visit to Russia when he was twenty-four: the occasion was the marriage of his wife's sister to the future Tsar Alexander III. Three years later he took his wife on an extensive tour of Europe and went on to Egypt to show her the places that had delighted him. The journey up the Nile this time took him into the Sudan. The Suez Canal was just nearing completion and he inspected it with Ferdinand de Lesseps who had designed it and was engaged in constructing it. It distressed him to think that Palmerston had not had the foresight to back the project but had left it to the French. 'It is our highway to India,' he said. On the way home they visited the cemetery at Scutari in Asia Minor where British soldiers killed in the Crimean war were buried. His Indian tour followed in 1875 and he returned home after visiting Egypt again and then Spain.

His zest for travel was unquenchable. There were recurrent and often long absences abroad even after he became King. No British sovereign has left the country so frequently and repeatedly. At least five times a year he crossed the Channel. An early annual event was his visit to Biarritz, usually in March. Then came his spring cruise in the *Victoria and Albert*: the Queen always accompanied him and sometimes this took them to the Mediterranean. It was a large and comfortable yacht with a crew of three hundred. Thirty servants in scarlet livery waited on their Majesties; the French cook, M. Menager, presided in the galley and was assisted by three master-cooks. The food was served on gold plate and a marine band played during meals. The cabins were spacious: in the Queen's sitting-room there was a grand piano; the King had an additional cabin for his uniforms and medals.

Recurrently there were visits to Germany, Denmark, Greece, again to Russia later in his reign, and always to Paris—he called there on his way out or on his way back almost every time he went abroad. Another annual fixture was his trip in August to one of the watering places on the Continent—it was Homburg at first, but later to avoid the crowds who followed him about he changed to Marienbad. He went to take the cure, but did not keep to the prescribed diet, for he was often seen eating an enormous lunch or dinner, and would then go for a long walk to work it off.

The King's grossly heavy weight and his general appearance gave one the impression that care was essential in both his diet and his mode of life. But that care he never exercised. He was always on the go, some of it because his official duties required it, a great deal of it because it brought him the diversions he sought—on the racecourse, at the gaming tables, at country house parties, with women and at the theatre. His diet was subjected to no restraint. He enjoyed good food and indulged in gargantuan meals, which indeed were normal at the time. His day began with an enormous breakfast—bacon and eggs, haddock, chicken or woodcock. At eleven he had a snack consisting of lobster salad and cold chicken. At lunch there were more than a dozen courses, including always chops and steaks, York ham, duck and chicken, with lemon sorbets to break up the solid richness of the meal. Even his tea was elaborate—he had scones, crumpets, tarts, and cakes. Dinner, by far the biggest meal of the day, ran to fourteen courses as a rule; and afterwards a plate of sandwiches and a quail or a cutlet were sent up to his rooms in case he got hungry while he pored over his State papers. There was wine—a variety of wines—with the main meals; brandy and liqueurs followed. His drinking was fairly moderate, but he smoked excessively—always large, fragrant cigars.

He suffered from gout. There were bouts of breathlessness, and from time to time he had a sore throat which developed into bronchial catarrh. Aware of his remarkable powers of recovery, he ignored the concern of his medical advisers. In February 1905, when he was sixty-three the attack of bronchial catarrh lasted longer than usual. He appeared to be losing strength and the doctors regarded his condition as grave. Then quite suddenly there was a change for the better. They sighed with relief, but were horrified when His Majesty insisted the next night on rising from his sick bed and going out to dinner. It was with difficulty that they succeeded in restraining him.

The next attack, a year later, was even more serious. Attributing these winter bouts to the fogs in London, the doctors begged His Majesty to leave town, but he refused. He must, he insisted, be in town in February to open Parliament in person. In the following year, again in February, there was a further attack, much more severe than in the two preceding years. His strength began to ebb. His nights were sleepless and gradually his condition got worse. He coughed ceaselessly and there was the fear that he might burst a blood vessel. His Majesty became acutely depressed and talked of abdicating. But a night or two later, surprisingly, he got better and in a week he was up and about again.

At this an analysis of the King's health was drawn up by his doctors. It was dated 23rd February 1907 and was issued as a State paper. 'It is obvious,' the doctors stated, 'that His Majesty's health, even when it appears excellent to the world at large, unfortunately always is in a somewhat precarious state, and that, whilst it must be devoutly hoped that his extraordinary vitality . . . may presage many more useful years of this most precious life, it cannot be gainsaid that either a more rapid progress of any of the degenerative changes now at work or an acute complication of any kind may bring about, apparently suddenly, very serious results.'

His Majesty managed to live for a further three years, despite his disregard of his doctors' warnings.

But his visits abroad now became more frequent and his absences longer. He went chiefly in quest of the sun. For Biarritz, the watering place on the edge of the Pyrenees, with the Atlantic beating on its bright tamarisk-crowned rocks, he had a great affection. But its drainage at that time was faulty and at the King's request the British Ambassador asked the French Premier, M. Clemenceau, if he could do something about it. 'Both this year and last year,' he said, 'the smells and effects of defective draining were so much in evidence that the question of a change had to be thought of.' Clemenceau did what was necessary and the King was able to return again and again to Biarritz until the end of his life.

At Marienbad he met many beautiful women taking the waters—Russian widows, American divorcées, Austrian adventuresses, and occasionally went for a drive with one of them, or had a quiet dinner in a secluded corner of the hotel dining-room. Sometimes he played croquet, pressing his secretary Sir Frederick Ponsonby to join in and make up a foursome. Ponsonby disliked croquet and, in the hope of not being asked again, he never lost an opportunity of sending the King's ball to the other end of the ground. 'This made him quite furious,' Ponsonby records,[1] 'and the beautiful Madame Letellier, who was quite a good player, begged me with tears in her eyes not to make him so angry, adding that she understood that courtiers always allowed monarchs to win. I replied that this was out of date and that personally I always made a point of beating the Royal Family at any game if I possibly could.' But Madame Letellier, who was the King's partner, he adds, 'was too good for us.' The King also did well. It was 'a very exciting finish and they just won on the post. To my horror the King said this was the best game he had had and that therefore we would have a return match the next day.'

No matter where the King was, whether at Marienbad, Paris, Moscow, Berlin, or even while cruising in the Mediterranean in the *Victoria and Albert*, official telegrams kept arriving and despatch boxes were brought to him at every port of call by King's messengers. He insisted on being kept informed by his Ministers of all their plans and it was his invariable rule that every document he received must be dealt with promptly. Hours were spent each day going through the Cabinet papers and other State documents. No monarch, it has been said with truth,[5] had ever before kept in such close touch with current affairs. His Majesty made marginal notes, dictated replies, sent off telegrams. The work had to go on.

Every report from the Prime Minister was studied with care and His Majesty administered a sharp rebuke if it happened to be unduly brief. While Parliament was in session he also received a report every night from the Leader of the House of Commons to tell him of the day's proceedings. The King insisted that each of these reports should fill four sides of a quarto sheet and eventually transferred the responsibility for them from the Leader of the House to the Home Secretary. This practice, begun when newspapers were not allowed to publish reports of Parliamentary proceedings, was abandoned by the King's successor King George V, who felt that the newspapers recorded them quite adequately.

Lord Redesdale, a close friend of King Edward's, has left this record of an evening he spent with the King: 'One night I was dining at the Club, after King Edward had come to the throne but before he had moved from Marlborough House into Buckingham Palace. He knew that I was in London for two or three days alone, so he sent over to ask whether I was at the Club, and, if so, to bid me go across to him. I found him in his private sitting-room all alone, and we sat smoking and talking over old times for a couple of hours. Towards midnight he got up and said, "Now I must bid you good-night, for I must set to work," pointing to a huge pile of familiar red boxes. "Surely," I said, "your Majesty is not going to tackle all that work to-night!" His answer was, "Yes, I must! Besides, it is all so interesting." And then he gave me one of his happy smiles and I left him. "So interesting!" that was the frame of mind in which he faced his work—he, the man who we are asked to believe could not be brought to attend to business.'[16]

The statement of Government policy read each year at the opening of Parliament and known as 'The King's Speech', His Majesty insisted should be sent to him well in advance so that he may have time to study it. This was something new, for Queen Victoria rarely opened Parliament during her long years of widowhood. After going through the draft of the Speech, it was the practice of King Edward to make suggestions, and sometimes alterations, which were generally, but not always, accepted by the Prime Minister. His Majesty also objected to the Press being told beforehand what the Speech was to contain. 'I am dead against any "inspiration" being sent to the newspapers,' he wrote to Mr Balfour's secretary. 'It is done in no country, probably not even in America. The King's Speech is drawn up by his Ministers, but if the Press gets hold of it before it is made at the opening of Parliament from the Throne it becomes a perfect farce.'

Then there was the essential but tedious business of signing official documents, which were so numerous that the strain was considerable. During the last years of her life Queen Victoria, with her health failing, had fallen into arrears in signing commissions for the army. The South African war greatly increased this total and on his accession King Edward found 5,200 commissions awaiting his signature. He insisted on signing each one by hand, but found it difficult to make up the ground lost. By April, that is to say after struggling with them for over three months, he decided to sign a hundred commissions every day 'till they are finished'. But even this he was unable to fit in with all his other tasks, and he agreed eventually to use a stamp, but this was kept in his personal possession and used only under his direct authority. By June 1901 the arrears were cleared and it was estimated that no more than 200 commissions a week would have to be signed by him in future.

There was in addition a vast amount of correspondence to deal with—personal letters to the Kaiser, the Tsar and other rulers, to ambassadors, to relatives and to personal friends, all these were written in his own hand. Also in his own handwriting were his letters to the Prime Minister, the Foreign Secretary, the Secretary of State for War and other Ministers, with comments on the papers and letters forwarded to him. But later he found it simpler to set down his comments on the documents he received and to hand them over to his secretary to write out as His Majesty's views, but carrying his secretary's signature. At times the King dealt with the problem briefly by telephoning the Minister, or if a lengthy discussion seemed likely, a summons to the palace followed.

Prerogatives that Queen Victoria had been ready to delegate, during her illness, for example, or because of her absence abroad, the King insisted on retaining in his own firm grasp. On the eve of his departure for the Continent during the summer of 1901 (the year of his accession) his friend the Duke of Devonshire, who was at the time Lord President of the Council, pointed out that it was customary, especially as His Majesty was to be away for some weeks, to arrange for another member of the Royal Family to hold meetings of the Council, if required. But the King regarded this as his sole right. He informed the Duke that if such an emergency arose he would himself summon a meeting of the Council and would return at once to preside over it.

CHAPTER 13

The People's Holidays Abroad

The King's numerous journeys abroad roused the desire in others to follow his example and every encouragement was given them by the travel organisations.

Those who had the money had already begun the delectable practice of escaping the bitter winter in England and making sure of the sun. As a rule they went to Egypt and spent three or four months at Shepheard's Hotel in Cairo, making excursions to see the Sphinx and the Pyramids; or they went on a cruise to the West Indies or the Canary Islands. The Canadian Pacific Railway urged people to go further afield: they could go by train to Vancouver, then cross the Pacific to Hawaii, Japan and China. The cost of these journeys was, of course, beyond the means of even the middle-classes, nor could they have stayed away from their routine activities for so long. Special tours at much more modest prices were offered them by the South-Eastern and Chatham Railway to the South of France, where the season was in the winter. The Blue Train with its card room and writing saloons and superb cuisine (one dressed for dinner) took twenty-four hours or more to get you there; the only alternative was the long way round by sea in a P. & O. liner bound for Bombay. You got off at Marseilles and took a short journey from there by train. The sun would almost certainly be shining, the *mistral* on the Riviera was disagreeable but you did not get it very often, and if some thought the sea not warm enough for a dip they could always walk along the front and look at the Duke of Westminster's yacht through a telescope, or cross to the Iles de Lerins in a boat, or watch the King of Sweden playing tennis with a Russian Grand Duke, or attend the trotting races at Cannes. Excursions into Italy were also possible: one might not have the time to get as far as Rome, but there was Bordighera and there was Genoa. Compared with present prices by train the cost was far from exorbitant, though it was of course beyond the working-classes. The waitresses, the horse-bus drivers and one's cook would have had to be content with a journey to Margate (once again by the South-Eastern and Chatham Railway) or to Herne Bay— the women lifted their skirts a few inches and paddled with bare feet in the water, the men folded the ends of their trousers to their knees. One had to have a bathing machine if one wanted to swim. Women changed inside it into a costume that covered more of the body than a frock does now, with sleeves down to the elbows and an abundance of lace and pleats even on the knickers which were allowed to be seen and ended just below the knee, and no one could emerge from the machine until the horse had drawn it into the water.

Those a little better placed would have gone to Weymouth ('The Naples of England') or to Ireland. Some ventured as far as Ostend for a few days, chiefly for the bathing and the gambling, or went to Calais or Boulogne on a day trip for the *hors d'œuvre* and the *bouillabaisse*.

Advertisements in the newspapers and on the hoardings encouraged one to 'Take a Kodak with you'. Many did. Queen Alexandra was an enthusiastic photographer. She took a course of lessons at the London Stereoscopic School in Regent Street: her pictures were well composed and she published an album of them in 1908 as a Christmas Gift Book in aid of charity. Some of the pictures are remarkably good. Among them is an amusing picture of her daughters paddling in the sea.

And of course there was always Paris for holiday-makers to go to. Even those who could not afford it often dreamed of going there. They had heard of Maxim's—it was mentioned in all the naughtier songs one heard in the music-halls, it figured in the title of play after play, and one read in the newspapers of the King sitting down to supper there with a group of gay friends. What a vision of enchantment the very name conjured up. The elegant tables with their bright, white napery, the ice-pails in which the champagne bottles lay with their golden necks tilted, the beautiful women in their lovely evening dresses, the Princes, the Grand Dukes, the bearded senators and the diplomats—and beyond them the bandsmen in red coats playing their intoxicating music. A gay, light-hearted evening never descending to vulgarity, the tastiest and costliest food one could find anywhere, and oh! what a memory to bring back. Englishmen and women of the upper classes went frequently to Paris. There was the Opéra, the Comédie Française, the shops, and the palatable change from roast beef and Yorkshire pudding and thin Windsor soup. There was also the Moulin Rouge where Yvette Guilbert sang her risqué songs and La Gouloue danced. Sometimes, on seeing Edward there, La Gouloue her hair cut in a square fringe, would shout ' 'Allo there, Wales'—he was always 'Wales' to her. He would laugh and praise her talent, then turn to Yvette to say '*Quelle distinction, m'selle!*' Once, when Yvette excitedly told him that she was to appear at the Empire in London, Edward remarked: 'A first-rate house—pays 14 per cent to its shareholders.' Yvette asked with surprise how he could be so interested in money. 'It's necessary to have a lot to be able to lose it,' he said.

Ponsonby describes an occasion in Paris when the King decided to have *déjeuner* at some restaurant at St Cloud, where there was a garden and groups of people eating in arbours round the garden. 'We were a mixed party, half English and half French.' Among them were Mrs Keppel and her husband. 'On each side of us were parties having *déjeuner*, and Alice Keppel became nervous as she said one of the men in the party on our right had a villainous face. She argued in a whisper that anyone could come in through the gate at the end of the garden, and wondered whether it was quite safe.' Just before his accession, while at the railway station at Brussels, Edward was shot at by a boy of fifteen who belonged to an anarchist club. He was quite unperturbed and jested about the bad marksmanship of his assailant. The boy was caught, but Edward asked the authorities not to punish him too severely: they let him off because of his youth. The Kaiser was more exasperated at this than the King and blew off his feelings to his uncle— 'the jury are a set of damned, bloody scoundrels,' he wrote.

Ponsonby tried to reassure Mrs Keppel that there was ample police protection in that garden at St Cloud, 'but she insisted that this could not be so as they would never have allowed an obvious criminal to be so near the King. She was convinced I had given the police the wrong name of the restaurant and that we were at the mercy of any apache who fancied robbery and any anarchist who loved assassination.'

At last Ponsonby got up and, pretending he was going to get his handkerchief from his overcoat, he went into the restaurant to see the chief of the police and asked him if he was satisfied with the arrangements he had made. 'He told me the gardener working by the garden gate was a police officer.' When Ponsonby described the man at the adjoining table who Mrs Keppel thought looked villainous, the police chief laughed: he is a *bon garçon*, he declared, 'one of the best and most trusted detectives in the force.' Mrs Keppel was reassured and full of admiration for the strange ways of the French police.

Not until the end of the Edwardian age did motoring become a means of cross-country long-distance travel. In the towns, however, motor-buses were already replacing the horse-buses, but Green Line motor-coaches came in much later. The only alternative to the railway was the bicycle (often, as in the song, built for two). Many took their holidays on bicycles. They visited the Lake District, cycled to the West Country and Scotland, and some even took their bicycles to the Continent. The Editor of the *Daily Express*, R. D. Blumenfeld, mentions in his fascinating diary[41] a friend who was setting out on a cycle jaunt to Paris and going on from there to Avignon, Nîmes and Arles, then *via* Marseilles along the Riviera to Genoa and Venice. 'I shall probably go too,' he added.

Holidays on foot was another alternative. Thousands went for long hikes, tramped the countryside, traversing fields, climbing mountains. Bernard Shaw and Bertrand Russell often did that, walking twenty miles or more in a day. Shaw generally took his bicycle, wheeling it for a time but mounting it at intervals, chortling as he shot ahead of the bowed, weary and often angry Russell.

Hardly any workers in those days had holidays with pay. They had to rely on Bank holidays and came in swarms from the East End of London, some dressed in suits and caps completely covered with mother of pearl buttons, assembled on Hampstead Heath and gave vent to a spirit of gay abandon by exchanging hats, the men putting on the large feathered hats of the women, who popped on their heads the men's little brown derbys; then, with their arms linked, they danced to the music of a concertina or a mouth-organ. Around them whirled the merry-go-rounds to a tinny, gasping melody, punctuated by the *crack-crack* of contestants competing for china mugs at the shooting gallery or at the coconut shies; while in another park, not very far away, gigantic cart-horses decked in blue and red rosettes lined up with a gay submission for their annual parade.

CHAPTER 14

Sport

King Edward always regretted that his upbringing provided no opportunity for him to participate in any youthful sport: he had not been to school, at the various universities he attended he was sealed off from the rest, he was excluded from the games they played, so he saw to it that his sons and their friends played cricket and football against local teams at Windsor and Sandringham, They were taught swimming. They went boating at Virginia Water and on the Thames. They were encouraged to form sports clubs.

The only sports to which Edward was introduced by his father were those that did not require the participation of young companions: he took him fishing, shooting, deer-stalking and fox-hunting—he also took him to Ascot for the racing. It turned out that horse-racing was the sport Edward enjoyed most. On the racecourse he was in his element. He wandered about with his field glasses, going from the stand to the paddock, his face beaming, his eyes dancing, happy and completely at ease. All ceremony was abandoned. He mingled with the crowd, stood aside to let others pass. They patted him on the back when a horse of his won and called out 'Good old Teddy! Teddy Boy!' He loved horses and went out at four o'clock on a summer morning in a brown suit and a brown bowler to see the gallops on the Heath or on Bury Hill at Newmarket. He often stayed at Moulton

Paddocks, Sir Ernest Cassel's house at Newmarket, or with Leopold Rothschild. There were lunch parties before the racing began and then he would drive on to the course, cheered wildly by men in frock-coats and top-hats and women elegantly attired, and even more wildly by the crowds in the lesser enclosures. Once a young woman was heard to sneer during such an outburst: 'Of course they cheer him. People of that sort are his friends!'; at which a very haughty, aristocratic old gentleman turned on her and snapped: 'So are we!'

It was, of course, not always so. After the Mordaunt divorce case he had a very bad reception at Ascot; but when later that day a horse of which he was believed to be part-owner won, the crowd cheered. 'You seem to be in a better temper now than you were this morning, damn you,' Edward said. This brought laughter and fresh cheers. With a smile the Prince raised his hat and lit a cigar. As Prince of Wales he had very little success with his horses and when his Florizel II at Epsom beat a popular favourite called Wherwell, belonging to Colonel North, the crowd was very angry. An anonymous contributor to a book of personal memories,[22] states: 'Two or three hundred people assembled in front of Colonel North's box, shouting out wrathfully: "You've been robbed, Colonel! You've been done out of the race to please the Prince of Wales!" Colonel North came to the front of his box, his face if possible a shade more purple than usual: "Silence, gentlemen! No treason!" he shouted angrily. "Three cheers for the Prince of Wales!" and they responded with a good-humoured laugh. But the criticism was repeated when Florizel II won at Manchester; he had been let into the handicap at too low a weight, the captious critics said, and was meant to come in first if he had to be wheeled home in front on a wheel-barrow; and it was not till Florizel II had won the Goodwood Cup, and had made a gallant attempt on three legs to carry off the Ascot Cup, that the English racing folk were fain to admit that the Prince had at last got a good horse!'

He did not pay fancy prices for his horses, but took an

interest in their breeding and training which he supervised himself. After 1896 he had a succession of most striking victories. By his death the total sum earned for him by his horses was £415,840. His own bets were relatively modest: the highest sum wagered by him on a horse was £600. He used to say that his most fortunate purchase was the dam Perdita II. He bought her in 1887 for 960 guineas and in twenty years he earned a quarter of a million through her. Two of her offspring, Persimmon and Diamond Jubilee won the Derby for him.

His first Derby victory, which occurred in 1896, was quite unexpected. Persimmon was not the favourite. The most fancied horse was Leopold Rothschild's St Frusquin which after the parade became a hot favourite and carried most of the bets. The race was essentially between these two horses. At Tattenham Corner they broke away from the rest of the field and came to the front. Neck to neck they ran all the way to the post and, as one spectator phrased it, Persimmon only won by putting out his tongue. It was one of the most exciting finishes ever seen. During the race the crowd on the hill rushed to the railings screaming encouragement; even men in top-hats and well-dressed women hung out of their boxes shouting for one or the other. As the race ended there was silence for a moment. Every field glass was on the judges' box for the result. When Persimmon's number went up on the board there was a roar of excitement that could be heard for miles. Instantly the pigeons flew up to take the result to the waiting newspapers. While top-hats and cloth-caps whirled in the air, the beaming Prince stepped out to lead in Persimmon and the acclamation became delirious.

He won his second Derby four years later (in 1900) with Diamond Jubilee. That was a great year on the turf for Edward. In addition to the Derby he won the Grand National, the St Leger, the Eclipse Stakes and the Two Thousand Guineas. Any wonder he stood so high in popular favour.

He did not race in 1901 because of Queen Victoria's death. But in 1909 he won the Derby for the third time—

it was the first occasion on which any English sovereign has won this historic race. His horse Minoru was the favourite until the last day. Then an American-bred colt owned by Louis Winans was regarded as a formidable rival. He fell, however, early in the race and the serious challenge came from Louviers. Once again, as with Persimmon, there was a neck-to-neck race down the home stretch, and again the two horses shot past the winning post seemingly together. After a breathless moment of suspense Minoru's number went up and the scenes that followed quite surpassed the delirium over Persimmon's victory. Even the policemen who were trying to force a way for the King to reach his horse threw their helmets into the air. The King himself took on their task. 'Make way for the King,' he shouted gutturally, shouldering his way through. Those nearest him seized his hands, others patted his shoulders and back. All round there were cries of 'Good old Teddy!' Then suddenly peers and even the jockeys added their voices to the crowds' and everybody began to sing 'God Save the King'. Tens of thousands sang the anthem together and many wept with joy.

After horse-racing the sport which appealed most to Edward was yachting, partly because he loved the sea, but largely because it involved racing and provided him with fresh excitement. He took it up fairly early in life, qualified for a Master's certificate under the Board of Trade regulations, and was well able to handle the yacht himself. Early in the nineties a new racing cutter *Britannia* was constructed for him on the Clyde. She was a vessel of 300 tons and outclassed all rivals: with her he won thirty-two prizes in forty-three races. He described her with pride to his son George as 'the finest racing yacht afloat'. But when the Kaiser arrived at Cowes with an even better cutter *Meteor II*, which he had got from *Britannia*'s designer, Edward was furious. Finding he had not the resources to take up the challenge, he sorrowfully gave up yacht racing. But Cowes remained for him a social occasion. He sold the *Britannia*, and later bought her back for sentimental reasons: for it was *Britannia*, together with his many successes on the Turf, that led to his being acclaimed as 'the greatest sportsman of the age'—and of that he was very proud.

He did some fox-hunting as a child and in his youth, but much preferred shooting. When he bought Sandringham the shooting on the estate had been greatly neglected and he spent a great deal of time and money on improving it. The preserves in time became famous. The sandhills were alive with rabbits; each season 10,000 pheasant eggs were hatched out and a great battalion of keepers saw to the rearing of the young birds. In the winter the house parties included at least four crack shots—at the end of the day the bag was always laid out for the King's inspection before it was sent to the game larder. This extensive game preservation annoyed some of his farmers, one of whom, Mrs George Crosswell, published anonymously an account of her quarrel with him, but the agent at Sandringham bought up and destroyed all available copies of the book.[64] The King also did a lot of grouse shooting in the autumn at Abergeldie near Balmoral, and other game such as quails, larks, cormorants, cranes, flamingoes, herons and merlins during his numerous trips abroad; unfortunately he indulged too in live pigeon shooting just below the Casino terrace at Monte Carlo, a sport that was widely condemned for its cruelty.

His travels brought such diversified sporting delights as pig-sticking in India, hunting wild boar and chamois in the Hungarian forests of Baron Hirsch, and going after crocodile on the Nile. India indeed provided the most varied and memorable of all his sporting experiences. Each hunting camp was the size of a small town and covered many square miles of forest. For transport hundreds of camels, elephants and teams of oxen were used. The camp-followers numbered more than a thousand. In addition detachments of Gurkhas and Bengal Cavalry were in attendance to guard the Heir to the Throne: it irritated him to find each tent he slept in completely surrounded by his guard. In Jaipur he got his first tiger and he bagged six more in the course of his very first morning out in Nepal. While hunting wild elephants he had a very narrow escape. The hunters were closing in on a particularly dangerous tusker when suddenly the elephant charged straight at the Prince, who happened to be riding in front of the others. He let the elephant come within twenty yards of him, then turned his horse and galloped round to the elephant's flank. The others in his party quickly closed in on the elephant and captured it. That his life was saved was attributed to his cool courage: had he turned and fled the elephant would undoubtedly have overtaken his horse and the rest of his party would not have been able to come to his rescue in time.[22] The Prince had a large and luxuriously furnished tent; he had a hot bath every night, changed into evening clothes and sat down with his friends to a large dinner.

He was not personally interested in cricket or football. Golf he took up late in life and was never very good at it. 'Not bad—for a King' his instructor used to say: he nevertheless had a nine-hole course laid out at Sandringham. He began to play lawn tennis soon after it was invented, chiefly to reduce his girth, enthusiastically at first, very sporadically as he got older. Croquet, which required far less exertion, he thoroughly enjoyed: it gave him an opportunity of asking any pretty woman he met at Homburg or Marienbad to join in the game.

Ice-skating, and especially ice-hockey, he loved. After their marriage Princess Alexandra would drive out to Virginia Water to watch him play in a match. His enthusiasm endured until the end of his life. At Sandringham whenever the upper lake froze he was always the first to put on his skates; and he invited his tenants and neighbours to form teams so that they could engage in contests in which he himself most eagerly took part. In the severe winter of 1894-5 he brought his Sandringham team to London and challenged the House of Commons to a match on the lake in the grounds of Buckingham Palace: he usually took the goal, but played back himself on this occasion; Balfour was in the opposing team.

His other diversions, not strictly classifiable as Sport,

were of the indoor kind. Dancing, of which he had always been very fond (his unflagging energy kept him on the floor until five o'clock in the morning), he took a less active part in after reaching the age of fifty—'I'm getting too old and fat,' he said. He went on dancing quadrilles, not waltzes, for some years, but gave it up altogether by the time he became King.

The milder activity required for practical jokes and horse-play nothing would induce him to abandon. It brought him a very hearty enjoyment, which found vent in his deep, chortling laughter. It was a schoolboy diversion that he might have outgrown had he ever been a schoolboy and been himself subjected to the pranks that could not be inflicted on him later in life because of his maturity and his station. To us it seems most pathetic that a fat, elderly man should indulge in the childish but persistent practice of emptying his glass of brandy over the head of an elderly, bearded man, who was ten years his senior, but Christopher Sykes, weak and always obsequious, invited the torment by giving no sign at any time that he resented it, but said most meekly: 'Just as Your Royal Highness pleases!' The words brought fresh gusts of laughter; the humiliation was repeated. This silly prank conferred on His Royal Highness momentarily the role of a comedian. It was he who had roused the laughter and it encouraged him to use the liquid custard pie yet again. One would have thought that his sporting pride would have prompted him in time to abandon this cruel practice.

CHAPTER 15

Motoring

Motoring, regarded at the beginning of Edward's reign as chiefly a sport attended by the possibility of adventure, developed so rapidly during that brief reign that long before the end of it the displacement of the horse was all but complete.

Horseless carriages were not entirely new. In the latter part of the eighteenth century Nicolas Cugnot was careering about France in a three-wheeled car, encumbered and disfigured by a large steam power plant, but happy at being able to travel at a speed of two and a half miles an hour. Shortly afterwards steam-cars began to appear in the streets of England and when railway lines began to crisscross the country-side sporting gentlemen with money preferred not to be confined to the iron tracks. By the eighteen-fifties there were enough steam-cars on the roads for the Government to decide on taking action. They passed a law to control, and if possible suppress, such vehicles. While on the roads, they stipulated, these steam-cars must be in the care of three engineers and must be preceded by a man carrying a red flag by day and a red lantern by night. The speed limit was restricted to four miles an hour. This law, known as the Locomotives on Highways Act, was passed in 1861 and it was not repealed until 1896—four and a half years before Edward came to the throne.

Meanwhile inventors on the Continent had been experimenting with an internal combustion engine. One was patented by Daimler in 1885, and Benz in the same year produced the first motor bicycle. A few years later the first motor-car appeared—a Panhard: it had its engine in front under a bonnet, as now; its chassis was much like the chassis of today; sliding gear transmission was used, with clutch and pedal brakes and a foot accelerator. In 1895 there were four such cars in England.

It was not long after this, with no more than a very few motor-cars on the English roads, that the red flag ban was lifted and the speed limit was raised to fourteen miles an hour. The roads were quite unsuited to motor traffic. They were dusty—even horse carriages raised clouds of dust. But would-be motorists were undaunted. Companies were floated for the purpose of manufacturing motor-cars. The price of those early cars was almost prohibitive, but they were bought and the first London to Brighton motor race was held on 14th November 1896. The following year the Automobile Club of Great Britain and Ireland was formed. *The Autocar* was launched to encourage the enthusiasts. Public curiosity was immense. Large numbers of people flocked to the Imperial Institute in London to see the first exhibition of motor vehicles, chiefly motor-bicycles.

The early cars frightened the horses on the roads and the cattle in the fields, killed hens and knocked down pedestrians. Shouts of anger followed the motorists, but they went speeding on, able to travel now at the astonishing speed of twenty miles an hour. From time to time they broke down. People going briskly by in carriages or on horseback cast a contemptuous glance at the immobile vehicles, a man lying on his back under each car, while groups of women, having alighted while the repair work went on, strolled about in their long dust-cloaks and voluminous motoring veils, or sat patiently on low stools by the roadside, knitting to pass the time. They were not, however, discouraged: it was a new sport and they were prepared to accept the hazards.

Lord Northcliffe (then Alfred Harmsworth) brought out

his *Motors and Motor-Driving* in 1902. In it he said: 'Motoring, for the word will have to be accepted and recognised, is . . . sport.' It could provide a form of land yachting, he stated; or it could be combined with other forms of sport such as fishing and shooting, since horses could not be driven long distances without being rested.

But London's streets had hardly seen them at all. At King Edward's accession the streets were exactly as Dickens knew them: the horse provided the locomotion as it had in the days of the Romans and of Boadicea. But in the course of the nine succeeding years one by one the landaus and victorias, the growlers and the drays vanished. The 7,600 hansoms that plied for hire were reduced to fewer than 2,000. By 1905 motor-cabs were introduced: they numbered only nineteen and were called 'Clarences'; by the end of the reign there were 6,397 motor-cabs and the name Clarence was no longer used. The first motor-buses appeared in 1904; by 1910 there were very few horse-buses left—one of these, which ran from Moorgate Street to London Bridge, was withdrawn in 1911, but others were still to be seen in the London streets as late as 1916.

The horse-buses were in a great variety of colours: the dark green ones of the Associated Omnibus Company ran from the Monster at Pimlico to the Angel at Islington, taking in Chancery Lane on the way; the blue ones went through Bond Street to King's Cross; the yellow buses served Camden Town; and Tillings ran a four-in-hand bus from Balham to the City by way of London Bridge. Passengers boarding the same bus at the same time every day got to know each other well and were on the friendliest terms with the driver. Narrow and precarious though the stairs were, with eagerness they struggled to attain the exposed seats outside, and the habit persisted when the earliest, equally small, motor-buses came in: often on that roofless deck the cold was piercing and when it rained there was only a tarpaulin apron to cover one's knees.

But the public's greatest affection was for the hansom cabs. These gondolas of the streets, as Disraeli called them, were the pride of London. In the spring, like the surrey with the fringe on top, the cabmen would bring out their gay tasselled awnings and attach ribbons and nosegays to their whips. They were a strange fraternity. They quarrelled with each other constantly and duelled with their whips as their cabs crossed, but towards their fares there was almost a fairground friendliness. 'Toss you, double or quits' was the recurrent offer at the end of a journey—and even when they lost there was a jest and a laugh.

Rotten Row was never the same again after the motor-cars took possession. The elegant riders, who touched their top-hats as they trotted past or pulled up to exchange a word or two with women strolling along the path in lovely creations and with gay parasols, began to diminish. Gone too were the magnificent landaus and victorias drawn by sleek horses, the coachmen wearing cockades, the footmen in livery, and the smart yellow or cream traps behind tandem horses. No more would straw be laid upon the road to warn coachmen to drive slowly because someone lay sick in the adjoining house. The costers' donkeys too began to disappear from the streets, but the drays and cart-horses lingered on. In time the fire brigade abandoned its horses and changed to motor vehicles. But Lord Rosebery kept on his cabriolet.

The mews where the horses were stalled fell vacant—years later they were to be converted into small attractive residences. The discarded horses were led to a mart in the Harrow Road to be sold at the rate of 150 a day while the stable-hands looked on sadly.

The growing motor industry, following the immense public interest in the exhibition held at the Imperial Institute just before Edward came to the throne, arranged for an annual Motor Show at the Crystal Palace. A curious exhibit at the Show of 1902 was the Simms 'War Motor-car' —a forerunner of the armoured car and the tank, designed, it was said, for coast defence. It was capable of attaining a speed of twelve miles an hour, which was as breath-taking then as a jet aeroplane with a speed of 2,000 miles an hour is now. This 'War Motor-car' was made by Vickers and

Martin. It was 28 feet long, bullet-proof, had a ram at each end, weighed six tons and was equipped with two automatic quick-firing guns and two pom-poms. Its travelling range, we are told, was 500 miles, which meant, of course, that once the petrol tank was refilled it could go on for a further 500 miles.

The internal combustion engine led inevitably to the displacement of the balloon by the aeroplane. In the early years of the Edwardian age, one of the diversions of the well-to-do was to go ballooning. They would meet at Ranelagh from where the Aero Club generally operated. For many it was a pleasant outing, like going to watch a game of polo. They sat down to lunch or tea and came out with their shooting-sticks and parasols to see the ascents.

Ballooning had come a long way since 1783 when one sat in a wicker-basket, cut the ropes and drifted at the mercy of the winds; by heaving out sandbags, carried as ballast, it had become possible to descend more or less where one wanted—generally in a field some miles out of London or, with less precision, in the branches of a tree. But by now the balloon had been converted into a dirigible: it was possible to steer and direct it. The steam-engine with which the early dirigibles were equipped (the first in 1852) had been abandoned because of the risk of fire, and electric motors were substituted.

In 1901, the year Edward came to the throne, Frank Hedges Butler formed the Aero Club and arranged for balloon races to be held, with a fifty-guinea cup as the prize. Seven balloons competed, rising from the lawns of Ranelagh Club, which was completely transformed and resembled, it was said, 'the enclosure at Ascot on Cup Day'—the women in the latest creations of Worth and Lucille, the men in top-hats, with carnations in their button holes.

It was a recurrent event and caused necks to be craned for many miles around London and for voices to shout excitedly 'Balloon! Balloon!' Parents pointed to the sky to delight their children. Farm-workers leaned on their forks and gaped. Then suddenly, to the horror of all, one of the balloons would begin to lose height, seemingly out of control. Open-mouthed they stared, wondering where it might alight. After a moment all would start to run across the fields, the more agile leaping fences and gates. A simple farm hand at Coulsdon in Surrey was alone when a balloon landed at his feet. He sprang back startled. Hearing a voice ask: 'Where am I?', he looked about him in bewilderment, then going down on his knees, his palms joined in prayer, he answered in a hushed whisper: 'If you please, God Almighty, it's Coulsdon.' The place was known for some years afterwards as 'God Almighty Coulsdon'.

Whatever vision of the future enthusiastic ballooners may have had—and some indeed envisaged its use for reconnaisance in war and for dropping bombs—the success of Wilbur and Orville Wright in America in 1901 when they got their aeroplane to travel a distance of 600 feet through the air must have roused some misgivings: few regarded it as more than a fluke: it may be repeated, they said, but heavier-than-air machines could hardly be expected to travel much further. Nevertheless the Wright brothers persevered and a a year later were able to keep their machine in the air for a full minute. By 1905 their achievement was really spectacular: the biplane, fitted with a very light motor-car engine, flew for thirty-eight minutes at a height of 850 feet and covered a distance of twenty-four miles.

In England and France the wildest enthusiasm was roused. A number of young men followed the example of the Wrights. Henry Farman, an Englishman, went to France in 1908 to take part in a flying contest: the prize was 50,000 francs (£2,000 then) for travelling one kilometre towards a fixed goal and back—and he won it. Shortly afterwards the Wrights arrived in Europe with their plane: King Edward, whose interest in all inventions was intense, journeyed especially from Biarritz to Pau to see a demonstration flight by Orville Wright.

In July 1909 the French aviator Blériot flew across the Channel. At Rheims, during Aviation Week that same year, Louis Paulhan, a Frenchman, remained in the air for

2 hours and 43 minutes; two days later Henry Farman beat that record by staying in the air for 3 hours and 5 minutes —it won him the Grand Prix. In the following year Paulhan won the *Daily Mail* £10,000 prize for a flight from London to Manchester with Grahame White close behind him.

H. G. Wells foretold that wars in the future would be fought in the air. But there was not sufficient faith yet in aeroplanes in military circles, for France and Germany went on building airships for use in war.

CHAPTER 16

The London Round

The lines dividing the diminishing old nobility of Britain from the successive waves of wealthy commercial invaders frequently get blurred: though viewed as a virtue in retrospect it is not so regarded by contemporaries. The *nabobs* home from India with their baggage full of rubies and diamonds were cold-shouldered at first but were accepted by the time the eighteenth century ended. The railway kings whose rise began at the crowning of Queen Victoria, the steamship magnates who followed on their heels, and then the diamond merchants from the Rand in South Africa who established themselves in the lovely houses of the aristocrats in Park Lane—they were luckier: Edward granted them an immediate entry into his set. An aristocracy of wealth—that was what he wanted. He laid its foundations when he moved into Marlborough House after his marriage: it came into full flowering during the nine years of his reign. In all they were a small community, numbering but a few thousand. They behaved in an ostentatious, crude, and vulgar manner in which the King participated most heartily, as no doubt his predecessor Henry the Eighth would have done, but the world had moved on five centuries since then and the behaviour was not by any means to the liking of all. Puritanism lingered in high places. Dowagers, seated in stiff satins and brocades under the new electric lights, with a large ebony telephone hanging in the hall, sighed for the quiet dignity and the glory that was fast ebbing out but still represented for them the England they loved. In time a few yielded, but not all. The old routine went on alongside the new. They maintained their 'at homes'. Their friends still called in their carriages and left cards, drawn out of the flat gold case in the golden mesh bag dangling from their wrists. Their daughters wore huge rosettes of Parma violets and carried tiny bottles of smelling salts in their reticules. But the world was changing: in time instead of smelling salts they would be carrying pep-pills, making sure to pop one into their mouths before they went out for the evening; and the craze for goggling at the few beauties of whom everybody talked (a craze the dowagers hated) would be whipped up by the ha'penny picture-papers and the gossip magazines and carried to even greater though less enduring heights by television.

Apart from the extravagant entertaining done by the very rich, life at that time was not as expensive as it has since become. For one thing the value of money was different. New seven-roomed flats being built in the best suburbs, with electric light and tennis courts, could be rented for £50 a year. At Edmonton it was possible to rent a six-roomed villa for ten shillings a week. Grouse and partridge cost 2s. 6d. a brace, long-tailed pheasants were selling at 4s. Yorkshire fowls at 2s. 6d. each, Irish fowls at 1s. 6d. Fish was much cheaper: one could get Scotch salmon for 2s. a pound, the very best soles for 1s. 4d., cod and haddock for as little as 6d. a pound. Tomatoes were 4d. a pound. In the restaurants one could get a cut off the joint for 10d. Champagne, sold on draught, was only sixpence a glass in all the West End bars—and it cost no more to drink it out of a chorus-girl's slipper. A man could order a new lounge suit from his tailor in Hanover Square for six guineas with an extra pair of trousers for a further 35s.[41] The top-hat, once made of rough beaver, had been converted into the glossy topper by Lord Hardwicke, a friend of the King's; one took it in to have the nap ironed every few days and gave the

Above A group of Edwardian chorus girls—the Gibson Girls

Left Vesta Tilley

Edna May, the great Edwardian star of musical comedy

Above Mrs Emmeline Pankhurst, being borne away by the police

Below Mrs Pankhurst and her daughter Christabel in their prison clothes

Prince Edward in a 12 horse-power Daimler with
the future Lord Montagu of Beaulieu, July 1899.

Below   Ballooning at Ranelagh, 1906

Opposite   Kaiser Wilhelm the Second of Germany

Marconi, pioneer of wireless
Below   King Edward with the American aviator
Wilbur Wright at the aerodrome at Pau, 1909

Winston Churchill as a
young Cabinet Minister

Below Sandringham in 1891

Prince Edward and Princess Alexandra with Alexandra's
sister Dagmar, the Dowager Empress of Russia

man sixpence. These toppers cost £1, though you could buy one for 10s. Ready-made American boots could be bought for 15s. a pair, the price for English hand-made ones was more than twice as much at £1 15s. A young bachelor could live well on £500 a year. Income-tax was only a shilling in the pound, postage was a penny and the stamps on cheques cost a penny.

The imitators of these men were the original Teddy Boys. R. D. Blumenfeld, who was Editor of the *Daily Express* at the time, describes them as 'young bloods from Tufnell Park and Acton and Tooting Beck'. They were mostly clerks from lawyers' offices and City offices. At five o'clock in the afternoon they would congregate in the Burlington Arcade in Piccadilly and ogle the pretty girls as they went by. They came dressed up in frock-coats, highly polished top-hats and lavender gloves—some even wore monocles. 'They stand tightly wedged together leaning on their gold and silver-mounted sticks, looking bored and imagine that they give the impression to passers-by that they are all heirs to peerages and great estates and are just out for an airing.' The shopkeepers complained that their presence in such numbers caused an obstruction and affected their trade.

Most of the underground trains then were run by steam. The carriages were filled with sulphurous smoke and the passengers coughed incessantly. But work on their electrification had begun and new lines were being laid, one of them, the Central London tube, financed by the King's friend, Sir Ernest Cassel: it drew into London areas to west and east that were still green with trees and far horizons. Quite rapidly houses went up, the metropolis swelled and got congested in the evenings, for wives came up to town now to have a snack in one of the new teashops being opened by Joseph Lyons and the Aerated Bread Company, called familiarly the A.B.C., and then go on to the theatre.

But there was diversion enough in the suburbs before the underground trains and motor-buses came. Every suburb, even those that were quite close to the West End, had its own theatre. There was the Camden at Camden Town, the Grand at Fulham (providing opera from time to time), one at Kennington, another at Brixton, and others still at Peckham and Balham, Stoke Newington and Crouch End, and of course the Boro' at Stratford. To many of these the entire West End company went with their more successful plays.

Although the Edwardian theatre is remembered for its musical comedies and the gay diversions of the music hall, quite a large number of the plays in the West End of London were straight plays—melodramas in many cases. One queued up for the upper circle and 'the gods' (the seats cost only a shilling—early doors in some cases threepence extra) to see Henry Irving in *The Bells* or *The Lyons Mail*, or for a French farce with pretty little women in négligées running in and out of bedrooms, like *Frocks and Frills*, which the King saw at the Haymarket. There were also romantic historical plays like *Sweet Nell of Old Drury* with Fred Terry and his wife Julia Neilson at the Globe—'an unsophisticated travesty of history', the critics called it. Of the more serious plays the three that were quite outstanding were by John Galsworthy—*The Silver Box* in 1906, *Strife* in 1909, and *Justice* in 1910—all of them powerful pleas for the underdog: they roused the fiercest enthusiasm and stirred the conscience. After the death of the King, Galsworthy's *Loyalties*, inspired, many believed, by the Tranby Croft cheating-at-cards case in which the King gave evidence ten years before his accession, startled the West End.

Playgoers saw George Grossmith, George Alexander, Cyril Maude, Connie Ediss, Gerald du Maurier, Gladys Cooper, Forbes Robertson, Martin Harvey, Ellen Terry, Marie Tempest and George Arliss. Aubrey Smith (who like Arliss became a film star many years later) made his début on the stage at this time in a play with Lillie Langtry called *The Degenerates*—the press described it as sordid and vulgar.

At Drury Lane there was a chariot race on the stage in *Ben Hur*: it was one of the very few American plays in London at the time. There were at least twice as many theatres in London then—the names of many are now forgotten, like the Terry, the Hicks (named after the actor Seymour Hicks), and the Princess.

Sarah Bernhardt, Coquelin and other famous Continental actors and actresses came over for a short season and presented some of their famous plays: a few even toured the provinces to delight audiences in Liverpool and Manchester and Birmingham.

Music lovers queued to listen to Kubelik and Fritz Kreisler play the violin, Melba and Patti sing, and there was of course also Caruso. You could buy their records and play them over in your home on a phonograph, in the form of wax cylinders, but the flat black discs of the gramophone displaced them almost completely by the end of the Edwardian era.

Then there was the bioscope. Moving pictures were evolved as a result of protracted experiments in Britain and the United States, and were only made possible by the invention of a sensitised celluloid film by Edison in 1889. Edison was hotly opposed to these pictures being projected on a screen. They were shown at first at fairgrounds—you had to peep through a hole into a dark box, one person at a time: Edison's argument was that if too many people saw the picture at the same time the novelty would soon wear off. They were eventually projected in 1895 and a year later the first film was shown to an audience in London at the Polytechnic in Regent Street. So far movement was all that films aimed to show—a train rushing at the audience at great speed, a boxing match, news-reel shots. In 1897 a film was made of Queen Victoria seated in a landau with a parasol, arriving at St Paul's Cathedral for her Jubilee thanksgiving.

For some years films were presented as the last item in a music-hall programme, so that those who were no longer interested in the novelty could walk out. But with the coming of pictures that told a story, shortly after Edward's accession, it became clear that the film was going to have a permanent place in the entertainment of the public. These early story pictures ran for only ten minutes—the first of them was *The Great Train Robbery*. Comedies followed, then stage plays were photographed from a fixed position in the auditorium and one was able to see Sarah Bernhardt in *La Dame aux Camélias*. The royal procession and other street scenes at the time of Edward's Coronation were filmed: later when this was shown to the King and Queen at Balmoral the flicker made their Majesties' faces unrecognisable. To correct this the projectionist at the end threw on the screen a still photograph of the King, but in his haste it was put in reverse, whereupon His Majesty bellowed through the darkness: 'Decorations on the wrong side.'

London's first cinema was opened in Bishopsgate in May 1906. Many enterprising *entrepreneurs*, not certain how far the public would support such a venture, rented empty basements in various parts of London and presented a series of films. The response was encouraging and before the end of Edward's reign more and more cinemas began to open in in the West End and others went up in the provinces. But the film being highly inflammable there were some serious accidents: at Newmarket in 1907 a woman was burned to death and 300 members of the panicking audience were injured; in 1908 at Barnsley there was a worse accident of a different kind: during a children's performance many were turned back from the gallery because it was already full. A congestion on the stairs where those going down collided with those coming up led to sixteen children being crushed to death and thirty others being injured. Strict byelaws were passed and had to be enforced by a vigilant management.

The piano had not yet been ousted from the home, though the gramophone, and much later the radio, were to take over the entertainment there. Boys leaving school at the age of twelve found ready employment as messenger-boys in short jackets and neat little pill-box hats at a few shillings a week, and as they went on their errands the streets were filled with their shrill whistling, broken off occasionally to supply a phrase or two of the song. Most of the melodies were from sentimental ballads such as 'If Those Lips Could

Only Speak', 'In the Twi-twi-twilight' and 'Her Golden Hair Was Hanging Down Her Back', with such comic intrusions as 'I Do Like a 'Snice Mince Pie' and 'After the Ball'.

Marconi had already begun his wireless experiments, but it was in the very first year of the Edwardian era that the first wireless signals were successfully transmitted across the Atlantic from Poldhu in Cornwall to St Johns in Newfoundland. As with motoring and flying and moving pictures, it marked the beginning of still another vital and far-reaching change in the history of civilisation. A year later Marconi was able to send wireless messages to ships at sea 2,000 miles away from his transmitter. So rapid was the progress that in 1903 the First International Wireless Convention was called and within four years wireless stations set up in the west of Ireland and in Nova Scotia were opened for use by the public. In 1910, the year of King Edward's death, it was with the aid of wireless that Crippen, together with his mistress Ethel le Neve, while fleeing after the murder of his wife Belle Elmore, were caught on board the Canadian Pacific liner *Montrose* as it steamed up the St Lawrence River. He was brought back to England, tried and hanged later that year at Pentonville.

A further and very considerable advance achieved at that time was through the widespread adoption of electricity. It completely transformed the streets of London by night. In the dim gas-jets and fish-tail burners of the West End vast crowds had groped through a half-light and the shops were in complete darkness. Electricity gave them an opportunity for window displays which were even lit during the week-end. Soon plate-glass replaced the tiny, often grimy, panes. The confusion of ironmongery, hats, shoes and corsets, too much for one to take in, made way for a small number of effectively displayed articles, with women's dresses on figures more realistically feminine than the stiff, crude ones that had stood cheek by jowl in a jumble-sale jungle. Electricity also improved the technique of stage lighting and brought into being a new and impressive artistry in the presentation of plays. Power-stations went up all over the country. The electrification of industry followed.

It was indeed an age of explosive invention and research. In 1901 the Diesel oil engine was produced. In 1905 Einstein enunciated his theory of relativity. Peary reached the North Pole, Amundsen the South Pole, Younghusband entered Lhasa, the Forbidden City of Tibet. The British Academy was founded in 1902. There was an abundant crop of laboratories for physics (including the Cavendish at Cambridge) as well as for engineering: in 1909 the King laid the foundation stone for the Imperial College of Science in South Kensington. The frenzied search for technological advance was timely for the world wide markets that had sustained Britain's prosperity in the Victorian era had begun to show signs of contraction.

These earnest activities in no way affected the gaiety and frivolity of the age. The extravagant, and at times eccentric, dinners still went on. There was, for instance, the Gondola Dinner at the Savoy Hotel in London, when the courtyard at the back was made water-tight, filled with water and transformed into a miniature Venice. The dinner-table was placed inside a gondola and covered over with a canopy of silk gauze. Around it, in other gondolas, the diners floated; they were served by waiters dressed as Venetian gondoliers while a troupe of mandolinists, brought from Venice, supplied appropriate music. Still another freakish dinner was given at the same hotel by a man who broke the bank at Monte Carlo. As he had won on *Rouge*, red was the only colour used in the decorations—the ceiling was painted red, a red carpet was laid on the floor, the waiters were dressed in red, even their shirts, ties and gloves were red. All the flowers conformed with that colour, and the food too bore the same tint—prawns, *queues de langouste, mousse au jambon, choux-rouges braisés* and so on, with strawberries as the sweet. The dining-table was laid out to represent a huge roulette board with thirty-five guests, each seated at one of the roulette numbers and the host at the number that had brought him success.[65]

It was also an age of many hilarious hoaxes, of which the most notable perpetrator was Horace Cole, whose sister married Neville Chamberlain, a future Prime Minister of Britain. The victim of one of his pranks was a Member of Parliament, who had been silly enough to boast that an M.P. could never be arrested. That very evening, while walking with the M.P. along Piccadilly, Cole slipped his gold watch into his companion's pocket and some moments later breezily suggested that they might race each other. Both set off. Cole allowed the M.P. to get ahead of him and then started hollering 'Stop thief!' Passers-by co-operated in the capture. The police came up. Cole said that his watch had been stolen and the M.P. was led off to Vine Street police station. There Cole explained that it was a hoax, but it didn't help. There were court proceedings and the M.P. had eventually to apologise to his constituents.

The most famous of Cole's hoaxes was to get four young friends to pose as Abyssinian princes—one of them was a girl, who later became known to the world as Virginia Woolf, the writer. Suitably disguised and accompanied by Virginia's brother, who took on the role of interpreter, they set out on a visit to H.M.S. *Dreadnought*, the new and most important battleship of the Home and Atlantic Fleets, both of which happened to be assembled at the time in Weymouth Bay. A telegram had been sent in advance and the Commander-in-Chief's Flag Lieutenant waited on the red carpet to receive them as they stepped off the train. The Admiral's launch took them to *Dreadnought*, where the Admiral himself and a guard of honour waited to welcome them. The band played what it believed to be the Abyssinian National Anthem (it happened in fact to be the Zanzibar anthem) and they were taken on a tour of the battleship. A salute of guns was fired on their departure. Photographs were taken, and in due course, when the hoax was discovered, some awkward questions had to be answered in the House of Commons.[66]

But nobody seemed to mind very much. The jest had been prompted by youthful high spirits. To it, as to everything

135

else that went on in Edwardian London, including a light-hearted disregard of morality, Mrs Pat Campbell's famous axiom was aptly applicable. 'You can do anything you please here,' she said, 'so long as you don't do it in the streets and frighten the horses.'

CHAPTER 17

The Other Side of the Picture

There is another aspect of Edwardian England that cannot be ignored if the age is to be viewed in its entirety. The affluence and the extravagance were confined to a relatively small section of people who owned vast estates or drew enormous incomes from various industrial enterprises spread over Britain and the scattered colonies. Wealthy tradesmen, like Sir Thomas Lipton the tea merchant and Sir Blundell Maple who had a furniture emporium, had for centuries been regarded as outside the social pale—it was unheard of for them to call at the front door until Edward threw it open to them.

There was a graded descent to the lower rungs. The middle class was ranged in varying degrees of gentility: those who were related to the gentry were concsious of the barrier separating them from the rest, but both were securely above the line at which the working class began.

Below that line the bulk of the population lived. Many, while in employment, managed to eke out a living, some rather better than others, but unemployment was the curse of that age as of almost every age since the industrial revolution. For those out of work there was no dole or State contribution of any sort other than what the workhouse might provide. It was the alternative all dreaded: wives were separated from their husbands; the anguish and degradation were heart-breaking.

Poverty was widespread and acute. Men like Charles Booth and Seebohm Rowntree were engaged in investigating this evil and the publication of their findings brought about an upheaval of both thought and feeling. A number of social workers, mostly women who were well placed themselves, went into the slums to do what they could to alleviate the suffering. They found families living eleven or more to a room, often eleven or more in one bed. Was private charity enough, some wondered? They felt it was not. In the view of others, who judged distress without any attempt at personal probing, the plight of the poor was attributed to improvidence or self-indulgence.

Booth's extensive and searching report[38] on four million people living in the poorer parts of London filled seventeen volumes in the new and definitive edition published in 1902-3. It showed that the actual poverty was great both in mass and degree. The word 'poor' he applied to those 'who had a sufficiently regular though bare income, such as 18s. to 21s. per week for a moderate family', and 'very poor' to those 'who from any cause fall much below this standard.' The very poor, he added, live in a state of 'chronic want'. Into these two categories fell more than a third of the four million people covered in his report. Those in employment, and so in a state of 'comparative comfort', numbered just over two million. Of the remainder 20,000 lived in 'common lodging houses', 20,000 in hotels and boarding houses, 96,000 were inmates of various institutions. The streets in these quarters were narrow and often blocked by barrows selling pigeons, canaries, rabbits, parrots and guinea-pigs. On the outskirts were movable shooting galleries and Aunt Sallies. Men could be seen standing up 'in dog-carts offering racing tips in sealed envelopes'.

In this squalid setting there was destitution, hunger, drunkenness, brutality and crime. Thousands of prostitutes lived alongside families who slept, cooked, mated and gave birth to children in the one room, which was often no more than eight feet square.[39] Dirt and vermin were everywhere. 'Several occupants have said,' Booth recorded, 'that in hot weather they don't go to bed, but sit in their clothes in the least infested part of the room. What good is it, they said, to go to bed when you can't get a wink of sleep for bugs and fleas?'

It was for such people as these, since many thousands of homes had no baths, that the more privileged, stirred by their conscience, began to build public baths; during the Edwardian era these were added to enormously by many municipalities. One in Manchester, elaborately constructed in 1906, with mahogany for its woodwork and a stained glass window of an angel (since cleanliness is next to godliness), was divided into two grades for each of the sexes: the first class provided a towel for twopence and allowed the user to turn on his or her own water; the second class cost only a penny, the customer had to bring his own towel and the supply of water was restricted.

The doors of the over-crowded, insanitary dwellings in the mean streets stood open all night and the passage and stairs gave shelter to many who were entirely homeless. There was only one water-tap and one closet for six or seven families, with a queue waiting, and the stench was appalling. Violence was common and sometimes led to murder. It would be wrong, however, to assume that only the depraved and the morally degraded lived in such dwellings. Surprisingly there were quite a number of men and women of good character and orderly habits, difficult though they must have found it to observe their standards of cleanliness in such a setting. Many hundreds of others, men, women and children, slept night after night huddled together on benches on the Embankment or underneath railway arches by Charing Cross Station and the Adelphi, covering their shivering, underfed bodies with newspapers to keep off the cold.

The King was aware of all this and of the efforts being made by the Earl of Shaftesbury to help the destitute during the latter years of the reign of Queen Victoria. In these endeavours Edward had throughout those years shown an intense interest and wrote and talked again and again of them to Disraeli: he was prepared, he said, to take part in public discussions and sit on Royal Commissions to try to alleviate the distress of these people. As early as 1878 he stressed how important it was to the nation to provide better houses for the workers, to ensure a sufficient water supply, and to provide for those who were old and without means. He took the initiative with regard to the water supply of the country by writing on 29th March 1879 to Disraeli (by now Lord Beaconsfield) asking him to receive a deputation to discuss this. Beaconsfield merely acknowledged the letter, but in the next Parliamentary session a Bill was introduced to replace the private water companies in London by a public Water Board. This smacked too much of socialism for the House to accept it, and it was not until Edward's accession to the throne that the Metropolitan Water Board was at last formed.

Edward sat on a Royal Commission for the first time in 1884 and served as an ordinary member. The Commission had been set up by Gladstone to inquire into the housing conditions of the working classes. Both political parties were represented on it and Edward suggested that Miss Octavia Hill, who had been a social worker in the East End of London, should also be a member. Gladstone was a little startled by the proposal. The 'novelty of appointing a woman' to serve, he said, 'may require careful consideration on the grounds of prudence before the principle is adopted.' It was not adopted, but Miss Hill was called as a witness.

Before the Commission was set up a formal motion had to be introduced in the House of Lords. Edward, who was present as a member of the House, rose and addressed his fellow peers. He had some days earlier, after changing into workmen's clothes, gone round with Carrington, who was similarly garbed, to visit some of the worst slums in Clerkenwell and St Pancras. They travelled in a four-wheeler with a a police cab following. His escort were alarmed as he dived into narrow alleyways, but he brushed them aside and was greatly moved by what he saw. He was about to give money to a poor woman who lay on some rags with her three almost naked children lying around her, but was stopped by

Carrington, who warned him of the consequences when others, hearing of it, came clamouring in a wild rush.[44]

He described the visit to the House in blunt and blistering criticism, and added: 'I can assure your lordships that the condition of the poor, or rather of their dwellings, was perfectly disgraceful'; and he urged that the Government should take 'measures of a drastic and thorough character'.

Queen Victoria was most apprehensive when he informed her of his decision to serve on the Royal Commission. Nervously she followed all the reports of the proceedings and not until the sittings ended did she breathe easily again. But soon the Prince was seeking still another opportunity to serve, this time on a Commission to inquire into the relations between employers and workers. She was relieved to learn that the Prince's offer was declined. It was explained to him that the discussions and the legislation that followed would draw him too closely into party politics. He was more successful, however, in the following year (1892) when a Royal Commission was appointed to investigate the relief, quite apart from the Poor Law, which should be given to destitute persons who were incapacitated from work by old age.

Edward insisted that the working classes should be adequately represented on the Commission. One such member, Henry Broadhurst, M.P., who had served with him on the Housing inquiry, was already on it and the Prince was eager to have yet another. Eventually Joseph Arch, who founded the National Agricultural Labourers' Union, was added: he was Radical M.P. for the north-west division of Norfolk, of which Sandringham formed part, and he always referred to the Prince as one of his constituents. Broadhurst was invited to stay at Sandringham and wrote afterwards that he 'left with a feeling of one who had spent a week-end with an old chum of his own rank in society'.

The Commission sat for two years and the Prince, despite his numerous other duties, attended thirty-five of the forty-eight meetings. He asked the witnesses many searching questions. One of the things he wanted to know was why the poor hated the workhouse. He paid a visit to the Lambeth workhouse to see for himself what the conditions were like and asked one of the witnesses, George Lansbury, later a Labour M.P. and a Minister in the first Labour Government, to explain what the objections were to workhouse food and dress. He also wanted to know what the cost of old age pensions would be if paid by the State. A fierce controversy developed over this. Many members objected strongly to State pensions. Party issues were involved and the Prince was precluded from taking sides. Two reports were issued by the Commission and the Prince refrained from signing either, but attached a note stating: 'I have taken the deepest interest in the long and laborious inquiry of the R. Comm. on the Aged Poor, the meetings of which I have attended as frequently as possible. In not attaching my signature to the Report I do not mean to express disapproval of it. I feel however that as the subject has now to a considerable extent become one of party controversy, both inside and outside of Parliament, it has assumed a phase inconsistent with my position of political neutrality.'

The acute suffering of millions in the midst of abounding wealth and unparalleled prosperity provoked many questions, but those seeking a solution found a series of obstacles in their path, due, it was stated, to the tangled undergrowth of vested interests. Short cuts were impossible. Here and there, by gradual stages, some amelioration was achieved, but the plight of the vast mass of human beings remained unchanged. The cure, H. G. Wells (in his novel *The Passionate Friends*, published in 1908) appeared to feel, was not economic but psychological: only by education and an adjustment of mental attitudes could those held in the grip of such degradation become responsible citizens, ready to play their part in the democratic processes to which, understandably, they were completely indifferent, convinced, in their dejection, that nothing could raise them from their inescapable misery.

Indifferent to their plight or to participating in any way in the democratic processes were those who lived in the new ever-expanding suburbs. They were cocooned completely in complacency and insulated from contact with poverty. Hobhouse in his *Democracy and Reaction*, published in 1904, said: 'Suburban villadom is a political and social portent the meaning of which has never yet been analysed . . . Politically it is a greater burden than the slums.' The dead weight of their respectability kept them from undertaking any public duties. All they were interested in was keeping down the rates. Kipling described them a little harshly as 'the poor little street-bred people that vapour and fume and brag', and again as 'the muddied oafs and flannelled fools'.

Hobhouse attempted to analyse their detachment:[40] 'We have ourselves coined a new abstraction: "the man-in-the-street" . . . is now the typical representative of public opinion, and the man-in-the-street means the man who is hurrying from his home to his office, or to his place of amusement . . . the man who has not time to think and will not take the trouble to do so if he has time. He is the faithful reflection of the popular sheet and the shouting newsboy. . . . To this public opinion of the streets and the tramcars it is useless to appeal in terms of reason: it has not time to put the two ends of an argument together; it has hardly patience to receive a single idea, much less to hold two in the mind and compare them. Equally futile is it to come before this tribunal with any plea for those higher considerations which men recognise in their quieter moods. . . . He knows already all about any appeal you can make to the better side of him, and he has long ago chopped it up in his mill of small talk and catch phrases and reduced it to such meaningless patter that the words which must be used have acquired trivial and lowering associations.'

Also detached, though they did not live in suburbia, were those of whom Galsworthy was writing at that time in his novel *The Forsyte Saga*, of which the first volume, *The Man of Property*, appeared in 1906.

The collective effort of all these people was needed if a change in the condition of the struggling masses was to come—and indeed it did in these same vital years of the Edwardian era, as we shall see.

CHAPTER 18

The King and His Ministers

The King, like his mother, was, basically and instinctively, a Conservative, but unlike her, throughout his life he seemed to prefer the Liberals. He got on well with Gladstone, whom his mother hated, and was blunt about the scant courtesy she showed her aged Prime Minister. He was more at ease in Gladstone's company than in Disraeli's; and Gladstone, for his part, so enjoyed being with the Prince that, despite his intense hatred of smoking, he occasionally smoked while with Edward. During the many years of Edward's friendship with Lillie Langtry, when all society seemed disposed to cold-shoulder her, Gladstone went out of his way to be courteous and even called on her, gave her religious books to read (which could not have been very much to her taste) and arranged for her to write to him direct by enclosing her letters in a second envelope so that none of his secretaries should see them. He tried to induce Queen Victoria to abandon her strict exclusion of her son from affairs of State, urged her repeatedly to appoint him Viceroy of Ireland, but she refused to discuss it. Unknown to the Queen, he passed on to Edward a great deal of secret information, especially on foreign affairs.

With Balfour, who became head of the Conservative Government at the time of the Coronation, Edward had not much in common. 'He is always so vague,' the King said. He felt that Balfour treated him 'with scant courtesy'. For his intellectual gifts and his erudite wit, the King had not much appreciation: he preferred a broader, coarser sense of fun—small talk, even puns. Balfour's detachment and mental aloofness irritated him. A cold formality marked their dealings.

At first he did not care for Sir Henry Campbell-Bannerman, the rather stout Leader of the Liberal Opposition, whose pro-Boer sympathies had strongly displeased the King; but seeing him year after year at Marienbad, where both went to take the cure, the King got to know him and like him: he was congenial, took a delight in good food and loved France so much that he often crossed to Calais by the morning boat for the sheer joy of having a French lunch. The King regarded him as a 'gay old dog' and told Lord Carrington: 'I like Campbell-Bannerman, and I think he is quite sound on foreign politics.' Carrington, himself a Liberal, replied: 'If we come in Sir Henry will make Your Majesty a first-rate Prime Minister and will furnish you with a good government.'

Writing of these meetings at Marienbad, Campbell-Bannerman states: 'I have seen a great deal of him and found him most friendly; I avoid him mostly on the promenade, but meet him at dinner and supper, and he asked me ten days ago to come and see him and have a talk, when he expressed his satisfaction at having the chance of a frank conversation on things abroad and at home, as I must soon be in office and very high office. Thereupon he discoursed with the greatest fulness on the state of Europe (Germany and France and ourselves; very apprehensive to put it mildly), Japan and Russia (not the new treaty*); India, Army; and, among other domestic things, Ireland.'[27]

Another Liberal to whom the King was drawn was Winston Churchill, who had been a Conservative but crossed the floor of the House in May 1904 and had begun to belabour his old chief Balfour to the immense delight of

* The Treaty which was signed at the end of the Russo-Japanese War in 1905.

His Majesty. Churchill jeered at Balfour and spoke of his 'disreputable shifts'. 'We have been told *ad nauseam* of the sacrifices which the Prime Minister makes. I do not deny that there have been sacrifices. The House ought not to underrate or deny those sacrifices. Some of them must be very galling to a proud man. There were first sacrifices of leisure and then sacrifices of dignity . . . . Then there were sacrifices of reputation.'*

Forgotten was the old quarrel with Churchill's father Lord Randolph and the challenge to a duel. A warm friendship had since developed between Edward and Lady Randolph. She sent him a copy of her son's book *The Malakand Field Force* which dealt with the war on India's North-West Frontier—Winston was in the army at the time. His Majesty was so pleased with the book that he sent an enthusiastic letter written in his own hand: 'My dear Winston,' he said, 'I cannot resist writing a few lines to congratulate you on the success of your book! I have read it with the greatest possible interest and I think the descriptions and the language generally excellent. Everybody is reading it, and I only hear it spoken of with praise. Having now seen active service you will wish to see more, and have as great a chance I am sure of winning the V.C. as Fincastle had; and I hope you will not follow the example of the latter, who I regret to say intends leaving the Army in order to go into Parliament. You have plenty of time before you, and should certainly stick to the Army before adding M.P. to your name. Hoping that you are flourishing, I am, Yours very sincerely, A.E.'[28] The letter is dated 22nd April 1898. Young Winston, then not quite twenty-six, paid little heed to the King's advice, for in two years he became a Member of Parliament.

Balfour, before taking over as Prime Minister from his aged and infirm uncle Lord Salisbury, had been presiding over the Cabinet for some years. There were clashes from time to time. On becoming King, Edward felt it was his responsibility and duty to assist the Government by a tactful

* *Hansard*, 28th March 1905.

use of his personal influence. He followed with a close scrutiny the activities and pronouncements of his Ministers and never hesitated to express his disapproval of their conduct to the Prime Minister whenever he felt it was necessary, nor did a personal feeling of friendship ever deter him from administering his rebuke. For example when Lord Londonderry, the Postmaster-General, who was a close friend of the King's, replied to an anonymous letter of criticism published in *The Times* in January 1902, the King immediately asked the Prime Minister to inform Londonderry that he must not reply publicly to anonymous letters.

When any action was taken in the Sovereign's name, however formal, the King at once wanted to know to what extent he was personally responsible. He refused to be regarded as 'a mere signing machine' as he phrased it, and attached immense importance to such discretionary powers as the Crown still possessed. One of these was the prerogative of mercy. Throughout the reign of Queen Victoria this had been exercised by the Home Secretary without any reference to the Sovereign. The King took a different view. He felt he was personally involved because petitions from prisoners under sentence of death or from their relatives and friends were often sent direct to him. The Home Secretary, Mr Akers-Douglas (later Viscount Chilston), informed His Majesty that the Crown had to be protected from public and parliamentary criticism which might arise over the handling of such appeals. While recognising this, the King nevertheless insisted on looking personally into them himself. An early instance of this arose shortly after his accession. A New Zealand soldier, serving in the Boer war, was found sleeping while on outpost duty; he was tried by court-martial and sentenced to death, but the sentence was later modified to penal servitude. On being petitioned, the King asked for a full report on the case and, after studying it, directed the immediate release of the prisoner, which was done.

Another instance of his intervention was in the case of Arthur Lynch, an Irish Member of Parliament who had surprisingly fought as Colonel of an Irish Brigade on the side of the Boers. He was arrested at the end of the South African war, charged with high treason and sentenced to death: the sentence was commuted shortly afterwards to penal servitude for life. A number of appeals were made to the King on Lynch's behalf, one of them by Thomas Lipton, who was a friend of the King's. The Government was prepared to release Lynch, but only on licence; the King, however, felt that a little more clemency should be shown. A personal letter from Lynch asked the King for a full pardon, but His Majesty was not prepared to go as far as that. Eventually a conditional pardon was granted, Lynch was released from prison and was given his freedom with certain restrictions. Lynch thanked the King for his 'magnanimity', and some years later asked if the restrictions could be removed. The Liberal Home Secretary Herbert Gladstone was prepared to agree to this request, but the King took a different view and expressed himself quite forcefully in his reply: 'The acts for which Lynch was convicted—of high treason, of fighting against his country and of having ordered the men under his command to fire on English troops—the King looks upon as belonging to the category of almost the worst of crimes. . . . If his offence had been simply a political one, the King would at once, and very gladly, have acquiesced in Mr Gladstone's recommendation, but he regards Mr Lynch's crime as being on a par with political murders, and, while fully recognising the desirability of conciliating Ireland by any reasonable act of clemency, to endeavour to do so by removing the few restrictions which have been placed on a notorious criminal, who has already been most leniently dealt with, is contrary to the King's conscientious ideas of what is right and just.' He added that he would be prepared to reconsider it a little later on, and after a year agreed to grant a free pardon.

These two cases, and there were many more during the reign, indicate how conscientiously the King undertook his duties and what a great deal of time he was prepared to devote not only to State papers, but to long detailed reports of trials concerning quite humble individuals.

Throughout the years Balfour was Prime Minister there was quarrelling and dissension in the Government. In 1903 a crisis developed over tariff reform. The abandonment of free trade and adoption of a preferential system to benefit the Dominions and the Colonial Empire, had been publicly advocated by the Colonial Secretary Joe Chamberlain. It immediately divided the Government. A great many Tories were vehemently opposed to it and Balfour only succeeded in holding his Cabinet together by being ambiguous as to which side he favoured. The Liberals, themselves divided on other issues, united at once in defence of Free Trade. The King's sympathies were entirely with the free traders. Chamberlain resigned from the Government in order to campaign for tariff reform. Unaware of this, five other members of the Government, who strongly supported Free Trade, also resigned: these included the Chancellor of the Exchequer, the Duke of Devonshire, Lord George Hamilton and Lord Balfour of Burleigh. Balfour thus lost in one swoop six important ministers.

The King had a great deal to say about their replacement. To some names put forward by the Prime Minister he objected and offered suggestions which were eventually accepted by Balfour. But this was not the only clash between the Government and the King. There was also the question of importing Chinese labour for use in the mines in South Africa; of this the King had approved, but he strongly criticised the phrasing of the *communiqué* which was sent to the Press. His Majesty regarded this as an 'irregularity' and received an apology from the new Colonial Secretary Alfred Lyttelton, but he insisted on a public correction and explanation as well. Further, there were arguments over the appointment of new Ambassadors, on which the King was resolved on having his say, and also over what might have seemed of small importance, namely the issue of a medal for presentation to the Sanitary Board of Hong Kong for anti-plague work. His Majesty sent a stern note— 'No medal should be struck or worn except as emanating from the Sovereign, and I cannot sanction the present proposal. The proposed decoration is simply *hideous*,' and he refused absolutely to agree to it.

Throughout the following year 1904 things got worse. There had been uneasiness and resentment in Ireland. The King, who took an intense interest in that country and was in favour of certain reforms, short of Home Rule, was gravely concerned. He had been to Ireland in the preceding year and had had a triumphant reception. He drove for miles in his motor-car, visited remote villages, stopped at humble cabins to talk to the people who had the vague impression that he was King Henry the Seventh. He travelled through lines of 'frenzied enthusiasm', the Chief Secretary said; 'he laughed, thanked us all and beamed enough to melt an iceberg'.[29] These fresh wrangles led now to the resignation of the Chief Secretary.

In the winter unemployment rose to an abnormally high level and distress was acute throughout Britain. When Balfour advised a postponement of the customary New Year honours list until the following June, His Majesty somewhat acidly asked: 'Will the present Government then be in office?'

On the 20th July 1905 the Government was defeated in the House of Commons by four votes. Balfour's resignation was expected but he refused to resign. At this the most violent abuse descended upon him, led by Winston Churchill and Lloyd George. His resignation was demanded. The loss of seat after seat in recent by-elections was cited, but Balfour, brushing aside this solitary defeat in the House, insisted that the only 'plain test is whether the House of Commons supports them'. The King was displeased. He felt that the implication in Balfour's remark was, not that the Prime Minister should act in consultation with the King, but that the House of Commons alone had the right to dissolve Parliament. He nevertheless advised Balfour to meet Parliament, which was then in recess. But Balfour disregarded the advice and eventually resigned on 4th December. This was regarded at the time as a masterly move. The Liberals, it was said, were too divided to take over. Many expected the King to try to form a coalition of free-trade Conservatives and right-wing Liberals. But His Majesty did not do that. He immediately sent for Sir Henry Campbell-Bannerman, the Liberal Leader, and asked him to form a Government.

It was by no means certain Campbell-Bannerman could command the support of the majority in the House of Commons. It was not even certain he would have the full support of his own party. The Liberals had been split for some time. Only recently Rosebery had made it clear that he was not prepared to serve under Campbell-Bannerman. The most brilliant Liberals—Asquith, an able and astute lawyer, Haldane, a brilliant scholar, and the eagle-nosed aristocrat Sir Edward Grey—had championed imperialist policies that were not at all in accord with the pronouncements of the new Prime Minister. Could they be brought together to serve under him? It seemed extremely unlikely. Without waiting for their answer Campbell-Bannerman kissed hands and assumed office. The King was particularly pleased. 'Nothing could be nicer,' he wrote, 'or more courteous' than the attitude of the new Prime Minister. Campbell-Bannerman thus became the first man in the history of Great Britain to have a clearly defined status as Prime Minister. Until now the Prime Minister had no recognised position in the Government other than as the First Lord of the Treasury. In 1903 Balfour indicated that a definition of his status was essential and by a warrant two years later it was arranged that his successor should be accorded this status and take precedence after the Archbishop of Canterbury, the Lord High Chancellor and the Archbishop of York, thus ranking fourth in importance after the Royal Family. This arrangement came into operation on Balfour's resignation.

The new Prime Minister now directed his attention to forming his Government. It was obvious that this could not be done without Asquith, Haldane and Grey. All three were prepared to serve, but only on the condition that Campbell-Bannerman went to the House of Lords as Prime Minister and left the leadership of the Commons to Asquith.

In this they were supported by Campbell-Bannerman's doctor, who doubted that the health of the new Prime Minister, who was seventy, would otherwise be equal to the strain. The King talked tactfully of this to Campbell-Bannerman, but could not persuade him to agree: the dissidents, however, finally gave in.

The King was concerned as to who the new Foreign Secretary should be. He favoured the appointment of Lord Cromer, but the latter, when approached, declined on the grounds of health. Eventually the choice fell on Edward Grey, who had served as Under Secretary for Foreign Affairs in Gladstone's last Government. The appointment was acceptable to the King as Grey's father had been his equerry and His Majesty was Sir Edward Grey's godfather. Asquith was appointed Chancellor of the Exchequer, Haldane went to the War Office and Lloyd George was given his first office as President of the Board of Trade. Another member of the Government was Lord Carrington, a close personal friend of the King's. That settled, Campbell-Bannerman sighed with relief and the new Ministers set out for Buckingham Palace in their cabs. There was a dense fog, but they managed to arrive. On their way back, the fog became a pea-souper and the Ministers, clutching their seals of office, had to abandon their cabs and grope their way somehow, feeling for lamp-posts and railings and colliding with others who were equally lost.

Many in the new Cabinet were already well known to the King, but there were others, some of them extreme Radicals without any respect for the Royal Family and often very critical of them. But the King did not let this influence his attitude in any way. At all times he showed them the greatest affability. John Burns, the most extreme of them all, was highly delighted with his reception by the King. As President of the Local Government Board (since merged into the Ministry of Health) he was the first working man to receive Cabinet rank. The King had found it necessary in the very first weeks to rebuke Burns for advocating the abolition of the House of Lords. His Majesty was in favour of the hereditary system since the monarchy itself was based solidly and squarely upon it. This issue was to play an increasingly important part during the remaining years of the reign.

Parliament was dissolved on 8th January 1906. The General Election that followed was disastrous for the Tories. The Liberals won 377 seats, the Tories were reduced to a mere 132. Balfour himself was heavily defeated at East Manchester, for which he had sat since 1885. The Liberals had a clear majority of 84 over all other parties in the House. But their position was a great deal better than this, for they enjoyed the support of the 53 Labour members (there had until now been only one Labour Member, Keir Hardie, who was laughed at for arriving in the House in a cloth deerstalker cap) and also of the 83 Irish Nationalists. The Tories had the support only of 25 Liberal-Nationalists. The Liberals thus had an overwhelming majority of 356 over all their opponents.

It was an unusual assembly of M.P.s. For the first time the majority of the Members of the House worked for their living. Their spare time was in consequence limited. The House used to meet from two o'clock in the afternoon until 7.30, there was a break of an hour and a half for dinner, and the House reassembled at 9 o'clock and sat until mid-midnight. This had to be changed. The sitting now did not begin until 2.45, the dinner break was cancelled and the session went on uninterrupted until 11.30. The reason for the earlier rising was to give members dependent on public transport the chance to catch a late bus or tram home.

It was felt that in these changed circumstances M.P.s should be paid. A private Bill was brought in for this purpose, but it was not until five years later that a yearly salary of £400 was granted in the Parliament Act of 1911. Most of the new members, and there were 300 who had never been in the House before, had bought top-hats—this was regarded as the correct wear at the time. A few Liberals, however, and some of the Labour members refused to wear them. The new Government had under its direction an

Empire spread out over a quarter of the globe—or, to use the phrase current at the time, 'on which the sun never sets'.

A new seat was quickly found for Balfour, much to the King's relief, for he did not want Chamberlain as Leader of the Opposition. Licking his wounds and reflecting on his party's defeat, Balfour declared that the result marked the inauguration of a new era. 'We have here,' he wrote to the King, 'to do with something much more important than the swing of the pendulum or old squabbles about Free Trade and Fiscal Reform.' It was in fact the stirring of the conscience of the country to which the Liberals were determined to give the fullest possible expression.

The King was not too pleased at the immediate elevation to the peerage of nine Liberals and of a further seven in the Birthday Honours which followed a few months later. Campbell-Bannerman described it as a strengthening of the Government's position in the Upper House, but others spoke of it as a blooding of the Liberal hounds after a long exclusion from power. It further angered the King that Lloyd George should at the same time be making attacks on the House of Lords. But all in all he liked the new Government. Lord Carrington noted in his diary later that year that the King expressed 'himself perfectly satisfied with Sir Henry (Campbell-Bannerman) and the Government, particularly praising Grey and the Foreign Office.'[30]

His relations with the new Prime Minister grew into a warm and close friendship, although there were moments when his Liberal policy exasperated the King. They met again in Marienbad that summer. Campbell-Bannerman had brought his wife, whose health had been failing for some time, but, instead of her condition improving, she died during her stay there. The King was deeply moved and, with many apologies for intruding 'on your great grief', took in hand personally all the arrangements for the funeral service, which he attended. Her body was brought back for interment in Scotland.

A formidable programme of social reform was launched straightaway by the Government. The King was not uneasy at first. He merely asked that he should be informed very fully beforehand of what was being done. But he found the Prime Minister's communications brief and inadequate. Plans were being put before the Cabinet that had not even been mentioned to him. He considered that they should have been discussed first with the Sovereign. He complained constantly about this and asked Lord Esher to look into precedents which firmly established the Sovereign's rights. Esher attributed the Prime Minister's negligence to laziness. The King, because he liked Campbell-Bannerman, was ready to make allowances for that. Nevertheless, he administered a sharp rap on the knuckles from time to time. He also objected to the contentious speeches made by some of the Ministers and said that they ought to be kept in better control. These rebukes referred in particular to one Minister —Lloyd George.

Among the reforms of the Government most favoured by the King was the reform of the Army. Haldane had a difficult task. He had to appease the Radicals by reducing the cost of the Army and yet make it more efficient. The serious set-backs during the Boer war had shown how disastrously inadequate was the organisation as well as the training of the Army. Haldane overhauled it completely. In addition to the Regular Army there was to be the Territorials, an auxiliary reserve force, which would absorb the Volunteers and the Yeomanry. It was to be composed entirely of civilians trained in their spare time and would number eventually fourteen divisions and fourteen mounted brigades, as perfectly equipped as the Regular Army. He foresaw that one day there might arise a need for the despatch of an expeditionary force across the Channel at short notice and he was preparing for such an emergency. In seven years the call came.

The Government's other reforms brought almost continuous conflict between the two Houses of Parliament. An early clash occurred over the Education Bill brought in to adjust Balfour's Act of a few years earlier which had roused the hostility of millions of Nonconformists. This powerful and impassioned section of religious opinion had always been closely linked with the Liberal movement and, as Lord John Russell said of them, had been responsible for the abolition of the slave trade, for electoral reform and for free trade. Now in the new House of Commons there were among the Liberal Members as many as 180 Nonconformists. Until Balfour's Act religious instruction in the State schools had been non-sectarian and confined to reading the Bible and offering prayers to God without bringing in any catechism. Balfour brought all schools into the State system, including Church of England and Roman Catholic schools, and the Nonconformists angrily refused to pay rates for religious teaching of which they disapproved. They were prepared to have their goods seized and to go to prison and indeed in the year following Balfour's Act 37,296 were summoned for refusing to pay this education rate, 1,580 houses and their furniture were seized and sold, and 80 Nonconformists were sentenced to imprisonment. The new Liberal Bill wanted a return to the old position, when religious instruction in State schools was completely un-denominational. This was most vigorously resisted by members of the Church of England and by Roman Catholics. Passed by the Commons, the Bill was mauled mercilessly by the Lords, and started the quarrel that was to rage until the end of the reign.

Conflict between the two Houses was nothing new. It had blazed at intervals for more than a century. As long ago as the days of the younger Pitt it had been found necessary to create new peers in order to get through urgent legislation that the Lords opposed. Pitt had 140 new peers created, adding that number to a House which at that time consisted of only 240 peers, of whom 15, being Roman Catholics, were not able to take their seats. Lord Grey in 1832 only got his Reform Bill through the Upper House by exacting a promise from King William the Fourth that new peers would be created if the Lords remained intractable. Gladstone, similarly troubled by lordly obstruction in 1884, contemplated abolishing the Upper House and was only deterred at the last minute by Queen Victoria from appealing to the country on this issue. Ten years later Lord Rosebery talked of the need for its abolition.

Campbell-Bannerman was prepared for the conflict. Shortly after becoming Prime Minister he severely chided Balfour for hinting that the Lords could be counted on to reject measures passed by the Commons with its overwhelming Liberal majority. Balfour's statement was made while the election was still in progress—at that time polling was spread out over two or more weeks and the results were announced at intervals during that period. What Balfour said was: 'The great Unionist Party (meaning the Conservatives) should still control, whether in power or whether in opposition, the destinies of this great Empire.' Lansdowne, the Tory Leader in the Lords (whose fag Balfour had been at Eton), worked closely with Balfour and always consulted him as to how the Tory peers should vote. Thus the will of the people, expressed through the ballot-box, could be negatived by the Tories who sat in the Upper House not by election but by hereditary right. It was a negation of democracy; it made democracy inoperable. Only the deep-seated regard for all that was hallowed by tradition made many hesitate to sweep away the coronet and the ermine. Preserve it, but let it not interfere unduly with the rights of the voters: to that view more and more veered as the successive clashes developed during these Edwardian years.

The King throughout showed exactly where he stood. While bound by constitutional rules to accept the advice of his Prime Minister, he strove on the one hand to curb the abusive attacks on the peers, particularly by Lloyd George and Winston Churchill and, on the other, he sought to make the Lords a little more conciliatory and co-operative. He was angry when Lloyd George dragged his name into the controversy by saying in a speech at Oxford in December 1906: 'If the House of Lords persists in its present policy, it will be a much larger measure than the Education Bill that will come up for consideration. It will come upon this issue—whether the country is to be governed by the King and the peers or by the King and the people.' His Majesty's wrathful rebuke to the Prime Minister brought the rejoinder that Lloyd George did not 'greatly err' since it would have been disrespectful to speak of the peers and the people without any reference to the King as Head of the State. His Majesty was not appeased, nor for that matter were the Cabinet prepared to accept that every reform that was distasteful to the peers should be rejected. Campbell-Bannerman made his own position clear. 'We do not intend,' he said at Manchester the following May, 'to be a Government on sufferance, or to act as caretakers in the House of a Party which the country has rejected'; and again in the following month at Plymouth: 'The British people must be master in their own house.'

The health of the Prime Minister, never robust, began to fail. The strain of these continuing battles was too much for him. He had a succession of heart attacks during the course of 1907. The doctors advised him to rest. He went to Biarritz, but soon after his return had another heart attack. The King, gravely concerned about the condition of his chief minister for whom he had a great regard and affection, called to see him at No. 10 Downing Street and shortly afterwards himself left for Biarritz. Campbell-Bannerman died in April 1908 and Asquith, who succeeded him, took the unprecedented course of travelling across France to His Majesty in order to kiss hands. Lloyd George succeeded Asquith as Chancellor of the Exchequer, Winston Churchill, a junior minister, took over Lloyd George's office as President of the Board of Trade.

The battle with the Lords now began in earnest. There was a quarrel over the Licensing Bill, which sought to reduce the number of public houses in the country. As many as 32,000, that is to say one third of the pubs in the country, were to be closed over a period of fourteen years. Drunkenness was rampant. One saw men and women staggering about the streets and hollering abuse in the vilest language. The temperance movement had been trying to stamp out this social evil for fifty years. In most towns there were temperance halls where social gatherings were held but no drinks served. In Bayswater, London, Dr John Clifford, the Baptist minister, opened a non-alcoholic tavern called 'The Clifford Arms'. Temperance lecturers toured the country denouncing the evils of drink; most prominent among them was Philip Snowden, a fierce Socialist who had just been elected to Parliament and was destined to become the first Labour Chancellor of the Exchequer. Indeed Socialists and trade unionists were strong supporters of temperance, proclaiming, as Snowden did, that 'drinking poisons the brains of the workers, reduces their physical strength, wastes their scanty means . . . and makes them more easily the prey of the sweater and the exploiter.' At that time drinking was not confined to certain restricted hours. Pubs kept open all the time and a workman could if he wished, and he often did, call at the pub in the early morning on his way to work and stay there for the rest of the day. It was causing incalculable suffering, especially to working-class families.

The Liberal Government's Licensing Bill was opposed by the many influential brewers in the Upper House. They and others in the liquor trade who subscribed generously to Tory party funds made it clear that they would withdraw their support if the Bill wasn't squashed. The King, fearful of the fresh impending clash, tried to persuade Lansdowne, the Tory leader in the Lords, to adopt a conciliatory attitude. But this their lordships were not prepared to do. They were smarting under the 'bitter experience' of having had to let through the Old Age Pensions Bill, which gave a State pension of a mere five shillings a week to those who were over seventy. The new fight became known as the battle of the beerage and peerage *versus* the Government. The Lords rejected the Licensing Bill by a massive majority; most of the bishops, however, voted for the closing of the pubs.

But even though defeated on this issue the Liberals had already in the course of two years changed much of the pattern of life in England and brought into being the social scene with which the present generation is so familiar.

Herbert Samuel, then a young junior minister at the Home Office, aged only thirty-six, set up juvenile courts for young offenders, stopped children begging and smoking in the streets, introduced probation officers and established the Borstal system on a permanent basis. Lloyd George merged and nationalised various private and public companies competing for business at the port of London, into a unified body known as the Port of London Authority. An eight-hour day was adopted for the coal mines, against the fiercest opposition.

More was to come, leading up to the final battle with the Lords.

CHAPTER 19

Edwardian Women

The invasion of business houses by women who came to work as secretaries and typists is believed by many to have begun during the First World War while the men were fighting in the trenches. Actually it began much earlier. In the latter years of Queen Victoria's reign women started clamouring for the right to participate in many of the activities regarded as exclusively the preserves of men. Those in the middle and upper classes were no longer content to sit at home and wait for marriage; for one thing, there were more women than men and in consequence many thousands realised that they would end their days as spinsters. It was not enough for them just to be governesses and school teachers. Florence Nightingale had blazed one fresh trail, and they strove for further outlets. In the seventies they had won the fight for higher education. Many had studied medicine and qualified as doctors, a few were even trying to enter the law courts. In the City of London and the business centres of the large provincial towns there were already a great many women: some came to work as cleaners in the early morning or the late evening after the men had left; in all the teashops, which Lyons and the Aerated Bread Company were opening in large numbers in every busy street, there were waitresses at the tables and elderly women in the pay booths; at the telephone exchanges women sat at the switch-boards, while others in business houses, wearing head-phones, manipulated the long coils and plugs of the telephone extensions; and, although men still arrived in top-hats to do the clerical work in the banks and commercial houses, a growing flood of young girls began in the Edwardian age to pour in through the doors to sit down at small desks, tap at the typewriters and to take charge of the filing system. Thus a vast transformation was already taking place in this era and fewer women were content to pursue the back-breaking labour of plying needle and thread in their own homes for a mere pittance from the garment manufacturers.

Even well-to-do titled women got tired of doing nothing. It was not enough to travel to unusual places, write books about their experiences, or, after the example of Queen Victoria and Princess Louise, take up painting. They wanted a better, more remunerative outlet for their energy and their talent. Viscountess Folkestone formed an orchestra of nearly forty: Edward attended her first concert a few years before coming to the throne. Lady Wimborne opened a shop in Bond Street for selling bibles. The Duchess of Abercorn had a creamery, Lady Molesworth a jam factory, Lady Angela Forbes a flower shop in George Street, off Portman Square, Lady Auckland an antique shop, Lady Burton and Lady Augusta Orr-Ewing ran hotels. In *Everywoman's Encyclopaedia* for 1910 there was a long list of women engaged in such activities.

Not all women were content with finding an outlet and an income. Quite a number wanted a say in the running of the country. As far back as 1869 they had begun to ask for votes for women. The National Society for Women's Suffrage was founded in that year: Florence Nightingale was one of its members. Two years later they won the right to vote in municipal elections, but in national affairs this right was denied them. John Stuart Mill took up their fight in his stirring book *Subjection of Women*. Petitions were presented to Parliament year after year. The Isle of Man granted them the franchise in 1880, New Zealand in 1893,

Australia in 1902. But England still resisted. Queen Victoria was most vehemently opposed to it. She spoke of it as 'this mad wicked folly. . . . It is a subject which makes the Queen so furious that she cannot contain herself.' Florence Nightingale, though a member of the Suffrage Society, would not sign the petitions, nor would the novelists Mrs Henry Wood, Miss Charlotte Mary Yonge, or Miss Mary Elizabeth Braddon. Even Gladstone, the great Liberal, was luke-warm and undecisive—he had voted against the Reform Bill of 1832, but he was a Conservative then: the women had expected more from him now.

In the Edwardian age the women's suffrage campaign came to boiling point. In 1903 Mrs Emmeline Pankhurst, tired of the complacent way women had been campaigning, launched the militant suffrage movement. She formed the Women's Social and Political Union in Manchester and brought it to London shortly afterwards. In October 1905 a group of its members went to the gallery of the House of Commons to listen to a debate on women's suffrage. Mrs Pankhurst was furious when she heard Henry Labouchere talk of the immorality that might occur when a man, seeking a woman's vote, visited her in her home during her husband's absence. She strode out of the House in great indignation, gathered her group around her in the street and began to address them. But as no meetings of any kind are permitted near the House while Parliament is sitting, the police soon moved them on. They reassembled a little distance away and were joined by Keir Hardie, the Labour M.P., whose anger equalled theirs.[42] That was the mild prelude to a series of vigorous and startling demonstrations which continued for years. These women, and others of their group, slipped repeatedly into the gallery of the House to shout 'Votes for women', unfurl banners and throw leaflets down on to the heads of M.P.s. Every effort was made to keep them out, but it was not always easy to identify them. The meekest little woman, seemingly up in London for a day's shopping, was apt to rise suddenly and cause an uproar. Grilles were fitted to the public gallery to restrict their activities, though not of course their voices. They then took to chaining themselves to the grilles with powerful padlocks and it became necessary for policemen to remove the grilles and carry out the women as well as the grilles before the chains could be severed.

These formed only a section of the suffragette movement which was extensive and numbered in all nearly 500 distinct societies. Mrs Millicent Fawcett was at the head of an intellectual group which included Lady Frances Balfour, Miss Eleanor Rathbone, who later became an M.P., and Dr Maude Royden, afterwards a preacher at the City Temple, and they were totally opposed to the activities of the militants. The King disapproved of all of them. He felt that women should remain the delightful, decorative creatures he admired, and he was not at all pleased when some of the women in his own set, the Countess of Warwick and Margot Asquith among them, got involved in politics—the Countess had become a Socialist and Mrs Asquith was in favour of women's suffrage, which her husband, he gathered, was not.

The hopes of all suffragettes ran high when Balfour and his Conservative Government resigned and the Liberals took over, for many Liberals had been ardently in sympathy with the women's cause. But to Mrs Pankhurst and her militants sympathy was not enough. She wanted to know what the Liberal Government was prepared to do. Four days before Christmas 1905 Campbell-Bannerman, the new Prime Minister, held a meeting of his supporters at the Albert Hall. It was thronged with wildly enthusiastic Liberals. Also there were Mrs Pankhurst and some of her militants. They interrupted the meeting with their shrill cries and hurriedly raised their banner, which caused some laughter because it happened to be held upside down. For the General Election, held in the following month, the militants concentrated on just one constituency. They selected North-West Manchester where young Winston Churchill, by now a Liberal, was their target. The opening meeting of his campaign was at the Free Trade Hall, with Sir Edward Grey in the chair. At question time Annie

Kenney, aged twenty-five, a cotton mill worker since she was ten and a devoted supporter of Mrs Pankhurst, rose and asked Churchill: 'If you are elected, will you do your best to make women's suffrage a Government measure?' Churchill did not answer. It is puzzling why he remained silent, for he had voted for women's suffrage in the House of Commons the year before. As the silence continued, Mrs Pankhurst's daughter Christabel, also twenty-five, raised the banner 'Votes for Women' which the militants always carried about with them.

There was an immediate uproar. A Liberal put his hat over Christabel Pankhurst's face and it was some time before order was restored. It was then suggested from the platform that the question should be put in writing and given to the chairman. This was agreed to. The question was now phrased differently. It asked if the Liberal Government would give votes to working women. The question was handed up. The chairman, Sir Edward Grey, read it, but still there was no answer. Thereupon the disturbance began again. The women started shouting: 'The Question! The Question! Answer the Question!' Some stalwarts strode in a body towards them and hustled them out of the building. As they were being dragged and carried out, Christabel Pankhurst said to the policemen who were dealing with her: 'I shall assault you. I shall spit at you.' Not until after the women had been taken out and order was restored did Grey rise. He then said: 'I did not deal with the question because it is not, and I do not think it is likely to be, a Party question.'[43]

Annie Kenney and Christabel Pankhurst waited outside and when the meeting ended began to address the audience as it streamed out of the hall. Both were arrested. Christabel was fined ten shillings with the alternative of seven days' imprisonment, Annie Kenney was fined five shillings with the alternative of three days' imprisonment; both chose to go to prison. Later, when he heard of it, Churchill went to the prison to pay their fines, but the Governor refused to accept the money. It was the first spell of imprisonment suffered by suffragettes and the militant group were greatly heartened: it brought in a large number of recruits. One of the newcomers was Mrs Flora Drummond, a tiny Scotswoman known later as 'The General'; another was Mrs Pethick-Lawrence, who together with her husband, an old Etonian and the son of a banker, became formidable fighters for the cause; both had money and used it unstintingly for furthering the work, and were ready to face imprisonment. Another new recruit was Mrs Despard, sister of Field-Marshal Sir John French, later the Earl of Ypres: she was tall, pale-faced, snowy-haired and in her sixties. She too proved to be a valiant fighter.

The public at this stage did not take the suffragettes at all seriously. They dismissed the exploits as stupid, childish pranks. Every music-hall comedian was certain of getting a laugh if he mentioned the word 'Suffragette'. In the clubs elderly men got increasingly irritated when they read of women chaining themselves to area railings and became purple with rage when they drove past a procession of women carrying the familiar banner. 'They ought all to be locked up,' they growled, 'or better still certified and sent to an asylum.'

In May 1906 the militants and the intellectual section of the suffrage movement combined to place their case before the Prime Minister, Sir Henry Campbell-Bannerman. Also with them were representatives of other groups such as the textile workers, the co-operative and temperance movements, and so on. Mrs Pankhurst's delegates, five in all, set out from Boadicea's statue on the Embankment and drove in a forage lorry decorated with a huge red banner with the words 'We demand Votes for Women' in bold white letters. Of the delegates, only one was a man, Keir Hardie, the Labour M.P.; Annie Kenney was dressed in clogs and a shawl, Mrs Wolstenholme-Elmy, who was over seventy, wore a bonnet over her attractive grey curls. Thus they drove to No. 10 Downing Street, attracting, of course, a great deal of attention on the way. Many stopped to stare, a few cheered, others merely scowled and walked on. The Prime Minister received them with great affability. Mrs Pankhurst, speaking for her group, told him that they were determined to get the vote and were prepared 'to sacrifice life itself' if necessary. The Prime Minister said frankly that he personally was in favour of giving them the vote, but some members of his Cabinet were opposed to it. Their thoughts immediately turned to Asquith, for it had been repeatedly rumoured that he was the sternest of the opponents in the Government, and the delegates promptly hissed. They drove from Downing Street to Trafalgar Square where, from the plinth of the Nelson Column, they addressed a crowd which soon numbered 7,000.

A few weeks later, when Asquith was to speak at Northampton, Mrs Pankhurst and her followers first held an open air meeting to protest against him, calling him the enemy of workers and of women, then she marched into the hall while he was speaking and was promptly thrown out. Four days later, they went to his London house in Cavendish Square. He was out and they left a message to say they would be returning. They called again two days later. This time they came with a body of East End women carrying flags. They marched round and round the Square while one of the militant leaders, Theresa Billington, went to the door and rang Asquith's bell. The police instantly pounced on her and she slapped one of them in the face. She was led away and Annie Kenney took her place. She managed to reach the front door and kept her finger firmly on the bell. She too was arrested, together with some other women. When they appeared before the magistrate at Marylebone Police court, Theresa Billington challenged his right to try them since the laws had been made only by men. She was fined £10 or two months' imprisonment. She chose imprisonment and was sent to Holloway. Annie Kenney also got two months, the others received six weeks each—all went to prison. The sentences were extremely severe, in view of the much lighter penalties imposed, at that time and since, for far more serious crimes. And though, in essence, these were political crimes, most of the sentences the women received, now and later, were not in the first division, but in the second and even the third division, which meant that they had to wear prison clothes, were separated from their companions, were not allowed to see friends or write—they were virtually denied all privileges.

When Keir Hardie protested in the House against the severity of the sentences, he was supported by members of the Labour party. But no Party at that time was wholly behind women's suffrage. Labour approved but only if it formed part of universal suffrage: otherwise, on the restricted property qualification then in force, the women enfranchised would in the main have been Tories. This was also the view of the Liberal Party—Campbell-Bannerman specifically stated that to grant the vote now would weight the suffrage in favour of the well-to-do and would not adequately affect working women. Certain Liberals, like Asquith, were totally opposed to granting votes to these 'female hooligans', as the Liberal Member for Burnley called them in the House. So Keir Hardie's appeal met with scant support. Herbert Gladstone, son of the great Gladstone and now Home Secretary, refused to modify the sentences. That afternoon, in an article in the *Evening News*, Mrs Pethick-Lawrence declared proudly: 'We look to none but ourselves. . . . We are not sorry for ourselves. . . . What we are going to get is a great revolt of the women against their subjection of body and mind to men.'[43]

Undismayed, they went on. They never let up. In October Mrs Pankhurst pressed the Prime Minister to give an under-taking that women's suffrage would be passed 'this session'. He replied that no further controversial legislation could be put through at the moment. The women retaliated by coming to the House of Commons the moment Parliament reassembled. They were joined by a large number of working women from the East End of London and, 200 strong by now, they invaded the Central Hall. Some of them climbed the plinth of one of the large majestic statues—it happened to be that of Sir Stafford Northcote. Others unfurled their banners and raised a clamour which subsided as Miss Mary

Gawthorpe, a young school teacher from Leeds, began to address them with her feet resting on Sir Stafford's marble boots. She was instantly dragged off by the police. Field-Marshal Sir John French's aged sister, Mrs Despard, at once took her place. She too was dragged off. Members of Parliament had gathered in curiosity and Mrs Montefiore called to them: 'Can you men stand by and see a venerable woman handled in this way?' But they remained unmoved. As the police began to seize the rest of the women Mrs Pankhurst got knocked down. Pandemonium then broke loose. Her supporters shouted angrily. The police eventually took away ten of the women. Each was sent to Holloway prison for two months. Mrs Cobden-Sanderson, the daughter of the great Richard Cobden, said sternly to the magistrate: 'I am a law-breaker, because I desire to be a law-maker.'

In order to evade the police they adopted disguises. Some dressed as waitresses and even messenger-boys, wearing tiny pill-box hats. 'They sprang out of organ lofts, they peered through roof windows and leapt out of innocent-looking furniture vans; they materialised on station plat-forms, they harangued the terrace of the House from the river, and wherever they were least expected there they were,' wrote Ray Strachey.[42] They broke the large new plate-glass windows of the big department stores. They slashed the painting known as the Rokeby Venus at the National Gallery. Again and again they were arrested. A banquet was given at the Savoy Hotel in London in honour of those who had served prison sentences. It was attended by Bernard Shaw and his wife, Mr Philip Snowden, and Israel Zangwill, the Jewish novelist. Annie Kenney, dressed in a pretty green silk dress bought for her by Mrs Pethick-Lawrence, was escorted to dinner by Miss Beatrice Harraden, author of *Ships that Pass in the Night*. They all honoured the toasts of 'The King', 'The Royal Family' and especially 'Success to the Women's Suffrage'.

But the more orderly suffragettes (who preferred to call themselves 'suffragists') got very tired of these antics, which they felt brought contempt on the entire movement.

Mrs Humphrey Ward formed an anti-suffrage society of ladies in 1908 and in the following year some men followed their example by setting up a 'Men's League for Opposing Women's Suffrage'—the two bodies amalgamated eventually. But their meetings only roused laughter and the ardent fighters for the cause answered by making mock 'anti-suffrage' speeches at their own meetings.

The Liberals were the chief target of the militants because much had been expected from them, and though they had the power to do it, they had done nothing. At every by-election the one aim of Mrs Pankhurst and her minions was to see that the Liberal candidate was defeated. The Liberals certainly kept losing seats, but the claim was far-fetched; it was nevertheless ironic that in the battle with the licensed victuallers, the suffragettes should have been found on the side of the intemperate. On Winston Churchill being promoted to the Cabinet, in the ensuing by-election, which was customary at the time, they went again to North-West Manchester and backed his Conservative opponent. Churchill was defeated and had to seek another seat. They opposed Bertrand Russell when he stood as a Liberal at a by-election in Wimbledon. A group of the women attacked Asquith with horsewhips. Churchill was assaulted with a dogwhip at Bristol. In a blunt reply to one of the non-militant organisations, Churchill said: 'My previous attitude towards this question had, like that of many other members of the Liberal Party, been one of growing sympathy; and on the only occasion when I have had an opportunity of voting on it in the House of Commons I voted in favour of the motion. I cannot, however, conceal from you that I have lately been much discouraged by the action of certain advocates of the movement in persistently disturbing and attempting to break up both my meetings and those of other Liberal candidates. I fully recognise that these persons are not representative of the serious supporters of the movement, and I can only urge those who do represent them to exert their utmost influence to repress the foolish and disorderly agitation which is in progress, and which, so long as it continues, must prevent me from taking any further steps in favour of the cause which you have at heart.'

The most memorable demonstration by the suffragettes was made a few weeks after King Edward's death. They assembled in a formidable group 10,000 strong and marched four deep from Victoria Embankment to the Albert Hall, with 'General' Mrs Drummond at their head riding astride on a prancing horse. Behind came the banner-bearers and a drum-and-fife band with Mrs Leigh, the first victim of forcible feeding, as drum-major. Next were the ex-prisoners, 617 suffragettes wearing silver broad-arrows, one for each conviction. Behind them were women in caps and gowns, hospital nurses, and a motor-car with Miss Rose Harvey in it wearing her prison dress. At the Albert Hall more than £5,000 was collected for the cause.

Within four years the First World War gave them the opportunity they wanted. They not only took over from men a vast range of activities, all of them urgent and essential, but joined the services themselves. Until then the militancy of the suffragettes saw no abatement. In the Derby of 1913 Emily Davidson threw herself under the hooves of the King's horse Anmer as it reached Tattenham Corner. She was severely injured and died shortly afterwards. Many regarded it as an unnecessary and mad sacrifice, but the cause had won a martyr. The country was startled and roused.

It was in 1918 that they were at last given the right to vote and to sit in Parliament, but these rights were restricted to women over the age of thirty. At the General Election on 14th December, one of them was elected to the House of Commons—the Irish suffragette, Constance Gore-Booth, daughter of Sir Henry Gore-Booth, who by her marriage was the Countess Markievicz. She refused to take her seat. Ten years later, in 1928, the right to vote was extended to all women from the age of twenty-one—it was called the 'Flapper Vote'. Thus at last full political equality with men was attained.

CHAPTER 20

Emergence from Isolation

During the long reign of Queen Victoria Britain had kept strictly aloof from all foreign alliances, despite the fact that during the Crimean war, relatively early in her reign, British and French forces fought side by side against the Russians.

The five major countries of Europe, however, were already grouped in alliances by the time Edward came to the throne: on the one hand there was the Triple Alliance, formed by Bismarck and the Austrian Chancellor Count Andressy initially as a partnership between Germany and Austria but joined later by Italy; there was also an alliance between France and Russia, which was designed to contain Germany by providing a threat from each side if Russia or France were attacked. France had cause for uneasiness: she had suffered both humiliation and occupation during the Franco-Prussian war, and had since been confronted first by a vast extension of Prussia's frontiers which took in all Germany, and then by the formidable Triple Alliance.

The change in Britain's attitude came early in Edward's reign. It was felt that in the rapidly changing pattern of power in Europe, Britain's isolation could no longer continue. The first alliance was formed with Japan in January 1902 to safeguard the interests of the two countries in the Far East. It was hoped that Germany might also join it, but the bitter feeling aroused by Chamberlain's anti-German speeches at the time made this impossible. Had Germany been included in the alliance it is possible that Britain's subsequent negotiations for a partnership in Europe with one or other of the two existing alignments might have been differently affected, but it is equally possible that it would not. There were recurrent instances, especially in the early years of Edward's reign, when the Kaiser's enthusiastic outbursts of admiration for Britain made it seem as though he at any rate desired it. But the current of feeling in Germany, in the newspapers as well as among influential politicians, was markedly hostile to Britain. The Kaiser's sentiments were echoed faintly and fleetingly for a time, then once again the bitterness and the hostility returned.

These emotions were too deeply embedded, their roots stretched back half a century to the marriage of the Kaiser's father Prince Frederick William, later Emperor Frederick III, to Queen Victoria's eldest daughter Victoria. The bride, only seventeen at the time, charming and keenly intelligent, was most cordially received at first. But Bismarck (not yet Chancellor but Prussian Ambassador in Paris) met her shortly afterwards in Berlin and noted: 'If the Princess can leave the Englishwoman at home and become a Prussian, she may be a blessing to the country.'* But that was not possible for her to achieve, for her father kept warning her in his letters 'not to be seduced . . . into approval of that which . . . the reason could not recognise as good or fitting.' She was outspokenly critical of German behaviour. Her husband's liberal sympathies were traced, not unjustly, to her influence. It led to conflict between him and his father and, inevitably, estrangement. It was not therefore surprising that she should have been disliked. Bismarck, during his long years of power, hated her. Her son Wilhelm, though he dropped Bismarck after becoming Kaiser, never modified his hatred for his mother. This intense feeling spread in time through Germany and found its focus on England.

Soon after coming to the throne King Edward received alarming reports of his sister's health and at once decided to

* In a letter to General Gerlach.

go to Germany to see her. With him he took his physician Sir Francis Laking. The only other member of the party was the King's Assistant Private Secretary, Sir Frederick Ponsonby. It was His Majesty's first journey abroad since his succession and he was a little irritated at finding it no longer possible to travel with the old ease and freedom. Despite the attempt to keep his journey secret, extra police were out and crowds had assembled in the streets to cheer His Majesty as he set out to board the royal yacht *Victoria and Albert*. He crossed to Flushing and was met by the Kaiser at Homburg, from where they drove together to Friedrichshof, which had been built at the Empress Frederick's wish like an English country house. The Empress was bedridden and it was obvious that she was dying. The presence of Laking was strongly resented by the German doctors who did not even talk to him.

King Edward stayed only a few days and left with a heavy heart, aware that he would not be seeing his sister again. With great secrecy the Empress sent for Ponsonby and asked him to smuggle her large collection of personal letters back to England. 'I don't want a soul to know,' she said. 'Certainly Willie must not have them, nor must he know you have got them.' At one o'clock that night two enormous boxes covered with black oil cloth were carried by four men into Ponsonby's room. He labelled one 'China with care', the other 'Books with care' and despite his grave misgivings managed to get them out of the country with the rest of his luggage. They were published twenty-seven years later, in 1928. The Kaiser, by that time a refugee in Holland, living in bearded retirement at Doorn, was furious and tried to stop their publication, but failed.

Just before leaving Germany, King Edward asked the British Ambassador to see the Kaiser and tell him that 'in the event of any divergence arising' between the German and British Governments, the King would be glad if the Kaiser wrote to him direct and he would do his best 'to smooth matters down'.

The Kaiser was delighted to hear this and a few weeks

later wrote to the King. It was a tactless letter. His Majesty was intensely irritated and sent at once for Baron Eckardstein, Secretary of the German Embassy in London, who has left a record of the interview. His Majesty 'commented on the Kaiser's assurances of friendship for England with a sarcastic "I hope that is so".' Then he read out parts of the letter. 'When he came to where the Kaiser referred to British Ministers as "unmitigated noodles" he laid the letter down on the table and said to me, "There, what do you think of that?" After thinking a bit,' Eckardstein goes on, 'I said, "Wouldn't it be best if Your Majesty treated the whole as a joke?" He laughed at that and replied: "Yes, you are quite right. I must treat the thing as a joke. But unluckily I have already had to put up with many of these jokes of the Kaiser's, and even worse than this one too, and I suppose I shall have to put up with many more." Then he went on: "Whatever would the Kaiser say if I allowed myself to call his Ministers such nice names! As you know I have for years had the greatest sympathy for Germany, and I am still today of opinion that Great Britain and Germany are natural allies. Together they could police the world and secure a lasting peace. Of course Germany wants colonies and commercial developments. And it can, after all, have as much as it wants of both. There is room in the world for both Great Britain and Germany. Only we can't keep pace with these perpetual vagaries of the Kaiser. Moreover, as you know, some of my Ministers have the greatest distrust of the Kaiser . . . I have always tried to dissipate this distrust, but after all one can't go on for ever. And the abuse and threats that the German Flottenverein and its organs are perpetually pouring on us are not exactly calculated to get rid of this distrust." Throughout the conversation the King was more irritated than I had ever seen him before.'

These ever-recurring moods of the Kaiser made it impossible to form the alliance with Germany which King Edward envisaged. Nor could Chamberlain's further outburst against Germany in October of that year have helped. To have joined Germany, and have thus become associated with the Triple Alliance, would in any case have been a grave departure from Britain's desire for a Balance of Power, so rigidly observed throughout the eighteenth and early nineteenth centuries. It would have confronted France and Russia with a powerful block of four powers; and whatever the assumption of Russia's strength with her numerically vast but untried armies, France at any rate, after her humiliating defeat by Germany thirty years earlier, could no longer, despite her subsequent very considerable colonial acquisitions, be considered the equal of Germany in military might: Germany was growing stronger all the time and had but recently embarked on a vast naval programme, a challenge Britain could not in any circumstances be expected to accept but which may have coloured King Edward's thinking: an alliance with Germany would prevent not only the ruinous cost of a naval arms race, but would avert a conflict that would be inevitable if no agreement was possible between the two powers. The Kaiser had himself voiced the precise sentiment King Edward had expressed to Baron Eckardstein. In that same year 1901, while he was in England for the funeral of Queen Victoria, the Kaiser in an unofficial speech at Marlborough House, which was still at the time the residence of King Edward, said: 'With an Anglo-German alliance, not a mouse could stir in Europe without our permission, and the nations would in time come to see the necessity of reducing their armaments.'[3]

It seemed to both King and Kaiser a not unnatural alliance at the time. There were family and racial ties between the two countries and no conflict had ever divided them. Feeling in England had run very high throughout the nineteenth century against Russia. Britain had kept a ceaseless watch on the North-West Frontier of India, with troops and artillery ready to thwart Russia's covetous designs which had long been apparent: there were difficulties over Persia and more recently a risk of war in the Far East over Port Arthur. Relations between Britain and France too had been far from friendly. There had been colonial rivalry, markedly so over Egypt, which was to come to a head before long over Fashoda.

The Kaiser continued along his erratic course blowing hot and cold at intervals. Suddenly he despatched a special envoy to King Edward to ask if the Prince of Wales (later King George V) could come to Berlin for the Kaiser's birthday celebrations. Then he offered the King the rank of Honorary Admiral of the German Navy. 'It would be a great honour to our Navy, though of course it cannot boast of any history or tradition like the immense fleet at your command.' But behind the scenes he arranged to see the Tsar on a yachting trip in the Baltic. The parting signal from the *Hohenzollern* was bombastic: 'The Emperor of the Atlantic,' the Kaiser said, 'bids farewell to the Emperor of the Pacific.' With commendable restraint the Tsar replied with the single word 'Goodbye'. Next, quite suddenly, the Kaiser announced that he was coming to England to be with his uncle Edward for his birthday on 9th November. He arrived the day before and went straight on to Sandringham. Tactlessly perhaps, the King invited Chamberlain to be there at the same time, or he may have done so on purpose. He also, quite deliberately, provided a very full programme: there was shooting, concerts, theatricals, indoor games, and of course bridge. When the Kaiser left, Eckardstein records that the King said: 'Thank God he's gone.'

Queen Victoria had very accurately summed up the Kaiser's attitude to Britain. 'Willie,' she stated, 'wants to be friends with us, but doesn't want us to be friends with anybody else'; and it was obvious, to the King at any rate now, though he would, of course, have discussed it with his Ministers, that a German alliance was no longer worth pursuing. A great deal of time had already been lost and if Britain was to depart from her isolation in Europe then she must look elsewhere—to France possibly. Their colonial differences could doubtless be smoothed out and the inestimable advantage would be to have an ally in control of the ports on the other side of the Channel. But such an alliance was not easy to establish. Hanotaux, the French Foreign

Minister, was the chief fomenter of strife and it was not until he was succeeded by Delcassé that the initial steps were taken. That King Edward played a personal part in smoothing the path is undeniable. He began his blandishments as early as March 1898, three years before coming to the throne. On his way to Cannes that year he stopped in Paris to see the President and later in a speech expressed the hope that there would be 'a pledge of cordial relations between France and Great Britain'. But within six months the two countries were almost at war over the occupation by France of Fashoda in the Sudan. Britain's restraint and Hanotaux's replacement by Delcassé led to an amicable settlement.

Although the principal credit for the *Entente Cordiale* is generally given to King Edward, one cannot overlook the conciliatory attitude of Delcassé, the ready co-operation by Lord Lansdowne, the British Foreign Minister, and the contributory spadework done by Paul Cambon, the shrewd and tactful French Ambassador in London.

Eckardstein, the watchful German Chargé d'Affaires in London, has left a revealing record of a dinner given by King Edward at Marlborough House early in 1902. After the dinner, as Eckardstein was about to leave, he was told that the King wished to see him in his study. His Majesty mentioned the failure of the repeated attempts to come to an understanding with Germany and added: 'We are being urged more strongly than ever by France to come to an agreement with her in all Colonial disputes, and it will probably be best in the end to make such a settlement.'[24]

In the Spring of 1903 the King undertook his first foreign tour. His plan, he explained to the Foreign Minister, was to set out in his yacht the *Victoria and Albert*, calling at Lisbon to see the King of Portugal and at Naples to see the King of Italy. The return journey, His Majesty said, would be overland: he intended to spend a few days in Paris. Lord Lansdowne did not approve of the visit to Paris: he was convinced that the King would not receive a cordial or even a respectful reception, for the French Press had maintained a continuous hostility towards Britain—even in the theatres there had been jests against Britain and a great deal of ridicule.

The King, however, was resolved on going to Paris and would not be deterred. He showed a wilfulness that startled Lansdowne. His Majesty refused to yield and would not be accompanied by a senior member of the Government but selected Charles Hardinge, an under-secretary at the Foreign Office. 'What struck me most during this first State visit abroad,' records Sir Frederick Ponsonby, who went as the King's secretary, 'was the fact that the King himself made all the arrangements and supervised every detail.'

Edward's arrival in Rome greatly disturbed the Kaiser, since Italy was a member of the Triple Alliance. King Edward dined with the King of Italy, then called on the Pope, despite Balfour's stern disapproval. Reports of the success of the visit so concerned the Kaiser that he immediately decided to visit Italy himself and set out for Rome with twenty trunks packed with uniforms. But by the time he arrived King Edward was on his way to Paris.

The Kaiser was confident that the Paris visit would be a failure. He had learned of the King's insistence that his stay in Paris should have the fullest official recognition—that was a piece of stupidity by his uncle which would only lead to humiliation and all the world would know of it. But a thoughtful act by the King proved of inestimable value. While at Gibraltar he had learned that the French President Loubet was on his way on an official visit to Algiers. The King ordered a squadron of British battleships to leave for Algiers and salute the President on his arrival there. The President was so pleased that he cut short his stay in Algiers and hurried back to Paris to receive the King.

This visit to Paris has been regarded as the most critical episode of his life. What would happen?—that was the taxing question on everyone's lips, not only in diplomatic circles in London and Paris but even in the streets and boulevards of the two capitals. As Prince of Wales he had always been most enthusiastically welcomed by the Parisians. But much had happened since then. The conflict over Siam in 1893 when both the French and the English sent warships to Bangkok, followed by the crisis over Fashoda and the intense bitterness of feeling in France during the South African war had seriously poisoned the atmosphere.

The King arrived in Paris on 1st May. He was met at the railway station by the President and they drove together to the British Embassy in the President's state carriage, escorted by cuirassiers and followed by a long procession of carriages. The streets were thronged, but the crowds were not very friendly. There were shouts of 'Vivent les Boers!' and 'Vive Fashoda!' Here and there some men took off their hats and there were faint, feeble cheers. It was disheartening and disconcerting. But the King, dressed in a scarlet uniform, his still golden beard only lightly streaked with grey, kept turning to the right and left, saluting and smiling: whatever their attitude he continued to be charming. Hearing later the remark 'The French don't like us,' His Majesty turned to the speaker and said: 'Why should they?' His good humour remained unruffled.

It was as well for that same afternoon, while addressing the British Chamber of Commerce, he made a felicitous speech that was featured in the Paris newspapers. He spoke of his frequent visits to Paris as Prince of Wales and of his great affection for the city 'strengthened by old and happy associations that time can never efface'.

'A Divine Providence,' he went on, 'has designed that France should be our neighbour, and, I hope, always a dear friend. . . . There may have been misunderstandings and causes of dissension in the past, but all such differences are, I believe, happily removed and forgotten, and I trust that the friendship and admiration which we all feel for the French nation and their glorious traditions may in the near future develop into a sentiment of the warmest affection and attachment between the peoples of the two countries. The achievement of this aim is my constant desire, and, gentlemen, I count upon your institution and each of its members severally who reside in this beautiful city and enjoy the hospitality of the French Republic to aid and assist me in the attainment of this object.'

At the theatre that night the house was full but his reception was icy. At the interval, however, His Majesty insisted on leaving his box and mingling with the audience in the foyer. He spotted the famous French actress Mlle Jeanne Granier amid the throng and going up he kissed her hand and said: 'Oh, mademoiselle, I remember how I applauded you in London. You personified there all the grace, all the *esprit* of France.' He was overheard and there was a murmur of appreciation all round him. The hostility began to melt. In whispers the crowd reminded each other of his great love for Paris and the French people. But it was not until the third day, when his stay was at an end and he was driving to the station with the President, that a remarkable change in public feeling occurred. From windows, from balconies and from the pavements they waved to him, blew kisses, cheered and shouted enthusiastically: 'Vive *notre* Roi!' He had won through. The Belgian representative wrote: 'His Majesty has been completely successful . . . Edward VII has won the hearts of all the French.' Sir Frederick Ponsonby, who was with the King, declares that the visit to Paris was the real purpose of the journey. 'Had he gone only to Paris it would have aroused the anger of the Germans, but to take Paris on his way back from Rome seemed only natural.' And, looking back on it later, he added: 'The visit to Paris always seemed to me to strain the limitations of a constitutional monarch to breaking point. The King went to Paris with no Cabinet Minister to advise him or to act as a liaison between him and the Government, and yet he reversed the whole policy of this country.'* The German Ambassador in Paris, Count Paul Metternich, did not take it seriously. He regarded the King's visit as 'a most odd affair and,' he added in his despatch, 'I know for certain it was the result of his own initiative.'

It was in fact an important first step towards the signing of the agreement between Britain and France that is known

* Letter in *The Times*, 10th May 1922.

as the *Entente Cordiale*. President Loubet returned the visit a few months later and came accompanied by Delcassé. It was from the discussions between Delcassé and Lansdowne that a general outline of the treaty began to emerge.

The most important sections of the treaty were concerned with Morocco and Egypt, the two areas where there had been the greatest clash of interest. Britain was prepared to recognise the French claims in Morocco and reciprocally France recognised Britain's sphere of influence in Egypt. Various other adjustments included French fishing rights off Newfoundland and the rectification of certain frontiers in Gambia and Nigeria, which involved the granting of about 14,000 square miles of territory to the French. It surrendered claims in one direction for compensation in another. It secured for Britain control of Egypt and safeguarded the Suez Canal, the highway to the vast Empire of India of which Edward was Emperor. For France it greatly extended her North African Empire, which stretched from the Mediterranean across the blistering, treacherous sands of the Sahara, dotted by forts and guarded by Foreign Legionaries, to the borders of British Nigeria and the Belgian Congo. It was not a military alliance at this stage, that came some years later. The initial treaty, signed on 8th April 1904, was just an *entente*.

Parliament was not sitting at the time. The details of the agreement were nevertheless published in full and Balfour, as Prime Minister, informed the House of Commons when it met that its assent was necessary, especially with regard to the ceding of territory. The King pointed out at once by telegram· that 'constitutionally power to cede territory rests with the Crown'. *The Times* published a strong article that same day, confirming this and quoting a stream of precedents. It was, however, too late now. The consent of Parliament had been sought and was granted and the King had to accept the loss of one of the last remaining royal prerogatives.

At the time the credit for the *Entente* was given almost entirely to King Edward and, although, as has been seen, the contributions made by Delcassé and Lansdowne were of the utmost importance, the French had no doubt of the vital part played by His Majesty. 'Any clerk at the Foreign Office,' the French Ambassador Paul Cambon said some years later, 'could draw up a treaty, but there was no one else who could have succeeded in producing the right atmosphere for a *rapprochement* with France,'* and M. Poincaré, in a speech at Cannes two years after King Edward's death, said: 'We cannot forget that it was King Edward VII who first encouraged, initiated, and pursued this friendly co-operation between France and the United Kingdom.'

The Kaiser and the German Government could not have viewed with any satisfaction this establishment of friendship between France and Britain. Nevertheless Bülow, the German Chancellor, declared in the Reichstag that the treaty did not seem to be directed against Germany and the German Government had no objection to it. The Kaiser said nothing and was believed to share the view of his Chancellor. But some years later, after the First World War, the ex-Kaiser as he was by then, took a very different view. He described it as part of 'the English encircling policy against Germany', which he blamed entirely on King Edward. British foreign policy before then, he said, had been fairly conciliatory towards Germany, but grew steadily hostile after King Edward's accession—the analysis was inaccurate. Russia, though linked by treaty with France, was not yet a party to the *Entente* with Britain. That was to come later.

It was early in 1905 that the German Government's true feelings about the *Entente* became apparent. Morocco did concern them: they wanted to have a foothold there themselves; and their resentment of any sort of agreement between France and Britain now began to express itself. They formed the resolve to break up the *Entente* at all costs. Their plan of action was to make Britain and France suspicious of each other. By developing a lack of trust between them it should be possible to separate them.

* *The Times*, 15th April 1912.

They made their first moves immediately after Russia's humiliating defeat in her war with Japan. Obviously France could no longer count on her as an effective ally. Nor could Britain be relied upon to come to France's aid, at any rate not at this juncture. For one thing the Conservative Government's position was extremely unstable. By-elections had shown that the Liberals were going to come in and the Liberals, a pacifist party, would not under any circumstances be prepared, the Germans felt, to add military clauses to an agreement made by the Tories and less still go to France's aid single-handed.

The first hint of impending trouble came with Germany's declaration that she was being encircled by France and her allies. Their next move was to question the settlement in Morocco. This would embarrass Delcassé, the French architect of the *Entente*, and would of course embarrass King Edward as well, which was the particular desire of the Kaiser.

To the surprise of everyone the Kaiser suddenly landed in Tangier. Before setting out in his yacht in March 1905, he made a bombastic speech at Bremen about 'world dominion for the Hohenzollerns' and added: 'We are the salt of the earth, but we must also prove ourselves worthy of this high calling.' The visit was very theatrical, which was precisely what he wanted it to be. On arriving he got on to a white charger, possibly because he felt that was what Napoleon and Alexander the Great would have done. But the horse was restive and the Kaiser found the animal most difficult to manage as he rode through the city streets. Later he soundly rated his Chancellor about the whole affair. He insisted that Bülow was responsible for the entire charade. 'Do not forget that you set me personally on the stage at Tangier,' he wrote, 'contrary to my own will, for the sake of a successful move in your Moroccan policy. I disembarked there for you, because the Fatherland demanded it, on a strange horse, in spite of the difficulty caused by my crippled arm, and it was only by a hair's breadth that that horse failed to kill me—me, your stake.'[4 & 5] Bülow turned on the Emperor at this. He declared he had not asked him to make a bellicose speech at Tangier. In that speech the Kaiser had said that Germany was determined 'to uphold the interests of the Fatherland in a free country. The Empire has great and growing interests inM orocco.'

King Edward was furious when he received details of the visit. He wrote at once to Lord Lansdowne, the Foreign Secretary: 'The Tangier incident was the most mischievious and uncalled for event which the German Emperor has ever been engaged in since he came to the Throne. It was also a political theatrical fiasco, and if he thinks he has done himself good in the eyes of the world he is very much mistaken. He is no more nor less than a political *enfant terrible* and one can have no faith in any of his assurances.'

Though the visit had failed, it was not the end of Germany's attempts to break up the *Entente*. The French Premier, M. Rouvier, learned from Bülow that relations between France and Germany would be greatly improved if they had as Foreign Minister somebody of whom the Germans approved. Rouvier knew exactly what that meant. Delcassé was too pro-English and, since England could not be relied on to stand by France, there was no alternative but that Delcassé should go. Pressed, Delcassé sent in his resignation. The President promptly asked him to withdraw it and King Edward sent a telegram to say that he would personally greatly regret his departure. The King, returning from a cruise, stopped in Paris and saw Delcassé. This was followed by an official note from Lansdowne to say that if Germany demanded a port in Morocco, Delcassé could count on Britain's support in rejecting such a request. The support was, of course, to be wholly diplomatic.

But it was not a port Germany wanted. The dismissal of Delcassé was necessary if the *Entente* was to be rent assunder. Once again pressure was applied—this time in a personal message to the President from the Kaiser, who stated that he would like to visit Paris and wanted to receive the Grand Cordon of the Legion of Honour. President Loubet replied: 'I attach too much importance to the continuation of M. Delcassé's policy to be able to associate myself with his dismissal.'

Delcassé felt it necessary now to seek more definite help from England. Lansdowne would not commit himself beyond a 'discussion' between the Governments of the two countries 'in anticipation of complications to be feared'.[33] But that was not enough. The French Premier, Rouvier, dreading German reaction if France drew any closer to England, went to see the President. His manner and his words indicated his purpose only too clearly. 'War is hanging over our heads,' he wailed. 'The Emperor can invade France within twenty-four hours. The worst eventualities are to be feared. If war breaks out, it will mean, within a couple of days, the outbreak of revolution in Paris and the great cities. . . . Delcassé must tender his resignation.'

Finding that the Council was not prepared to support him, Delcassé resigned for a second time. The French Government had yielded to German pressure and Balfour, writing to the King, pointed out that France could no longer be trusted because of her surrender under threats at a critical moment of the negotiation. The result is, said Lord Lansdowne, that the *Entente* is quoted at a much lower price than it was a fortnight ago. At Marienbad on his annual visit that year King Edward refused to meet the Kaiser and when a member of the Kaiser's court urged him to agree to a meeting, the King regarded it 'as a piece of impertinence'.

It was not very long after this that the Liberals came into power. That their policy would be opposed to any military entanglement had already been made clear. The new Foreign Secretary Sir Edward Grey, like the new Prime Minister, was anxious to be on the best of terms with Germany, and Morley had warned the Viceroy in India to maintain friendly relations with Russia and avoid anything that might smack of militarism. Their embarrassment can therefore be imagined when, a few days after taking office and with the General Election in the offing, the French Ambassador Paul Cambon informed Grey that the Kaiser was still pursuing 'a very dangerous policy': he was insisting that a conference should be held at Algeciras to decide on the future of Morocco. Lansdowne had known of this. It had

not at the time been considered necessary to discuss the possibility of war, but it was obvious now that this would have to be
faced. It was of the utmost importance, Paul Cambon said, that
the French Government should know beforehand whether,
in the event of German aggression against France, Great
Britain would be prepared to give France armed assistance.

Grey replied that it was not possible to give an immediate
answer. The Cabinet had already dispersed for the General
Election and what the feeling in the country would be could
not be known until after the result. But he was prepared,
he said, to give a purely personal opinion. If Germany forced
a war on France with the intention of destroying the *Entente*,
then public opinion, he felt, would be strongly in favour of
France, and Britain would find it necessary to come to her
aid.[33] Grey added that he could not give a specific under-
taking on this without Cabinet support, but considered it
right that Germany should be informed of it; and he himself
warned the German Ambassador in London, Herr von
Metternich, that if there was war between Germany and
France, England would find herself involved. He thus went
much further than Lansdowne or Balfour had been prepared
to go. He even agreed that the military discussions between
the General Staffs of Britain and France should be continued
with a view to preparing for eventual co-operation, since
any last-minute improvisation would be disastrous. That
King Edward played some part in this is obvious from the
record of a conversation Paul Cambon had with the King
early that January. 'Tell us,' the King said, 'what you wish
on each point, and we will support you without restriction
or reserve.'[5] He had prefaced this a little earlier by very
wisely arranging a demonstration of friendship between
the two countries: he suggested that there should be an
exchange of visits by the French fleet and the British fleet.
It had the effect desired. As the British Atlantic fleet, led
by H.M.S. *King Edward VII*, entered Brest, the French people
gave it a wild, almost hysterical welcome. Many men and
women wept with joy as they waved and shouted in excitement. It was a most moving reaction to the recent

German bullying. Equally enthusiastic was the reception of the French fleet by the people of Portsmouth. Both King Edward and Queen Alexandra were there. His Majesty reviewed the fleet and afterwards he and the Queen received the Admiral and his officers on board the royal yacht. The French naval officers and staff were also entertained at Windsor Castle, at the Guildhall and at Westminster Hall by both Houses of Parliament. The Kaiser was livid and grumbled a great deal about his uncle 'prostituting himself' before the French.

The Algeciras conference was a dismal failure for Germany. France, with British support, triumphed all along the line. War had been averted, but Winston Churchill noted that these incidents marked 'the first milestone to Armageddon'.

Encouraged by this diplomatic success against Germany, thoughts turned immediately to converting the *Entente Cordiale* into a *Triple Entente* by the inclusion of Russia. Sir Arthur Nicolson, who had been the British delegate at Algeciras, was sent as Ambassador to Russia and King Edward promised to help him in overcoming such obstacles as stood in the way: these included hostility to the Anglo-Japanese alliance and the opposition in Britain to the autocratic rule of the Tsar. But when Grey suggested that the King should himself go to Russia and talk to the Tsar, His Majesty was shrewd enough to refuse. 'I honestly confess,' he wrote to Charles Hardinge, 'that I can see no particular object in visiting the Emperor this year. The country (Russia) is in a very unsettled state and will, I fear, not improve for some time to come. I hardly think that the country at home would much approve of my going there for a while. I have no wish to play the part of the German Emperor who always meddles in other people's business.'[5] But later that year, 'entirely on King Edward's initiative', writes Hardinge, a meeting was arranged in London between the King and Isvolsky, the Russian Foreign Minister. It helped to smooth out differences between the two countries over Persia, Afghanistan and Tibet. An agreement was signed in August 1907 and the King's visit to Russia in the following year to see his nephew finally set the seal on the *Triple Entente*.

CHAPTER 21

The Lords Battle

The battle between the Liberal Government and the House of Lords moved in the succeeding years to its inevitable climax. Too many Bills had been rejected or mauled out of all recognition. It was obvious this could not go on. The Liberals were finding it impossible to carry out their programme of reforms.

The foremost and most formidable figure in the culminating campaign was Lloyd George, with Winston Churchill as an eager and brilliant lieutenant. All the venom of their lordships and the Tories in press and on platform was directed at Lloyd George. Nor did Winston Churchill escape: against him was levelled a more embittered abuse, because of his aristocratic background and 'his treacherous role as a turncoat'.

Churchill was the youngest member of the Cabinet. His work as a reformer, overshadowed as it was by the work of Lloyd George and the others, has been generally forgotten, but his contribution was considerable. For example, having met William Beveridge,* then only twenty-seven and engaged in investigating the poverty and unemployment in the slums, Churchill created a special post for him at the Board of Trade with a view to alleviating the appalling conditions. Together they set up a vast network of labour

* Later Lord Beveridge.

exchanges. Until then hardly any existed. The unemployed had to spend their time trudging the streets and going from factory to factory looking for work. The labour exchanges served as a clearing house. They gave the men information about available jobs and told employers which men were suitable. They have since become a permanent feature in the lives of the people; on their foundations the welfare state was raised.

Churchill's attention was next turned to the evil of sweated labour, which flourished so abundantly in the slum dwellings of East London and other cities. For the pitiful sum of a penny an hour women, children and cripples laboured in their own miserable rooms, stitching garments, making boxes, sticking labels. These workers had no trade unions to protect them. In 1908 the Liberal newspaper the *Daily News*, founded more than half a century before by Charles Dickens, held two Sweated Trades Exhibitions in London, which shocked and roused the people. Churchill acted by setting up Boards to regulate the wages of the 200,000 workers involved and gradually an improvement was achieved in their conditions.

But the major reforms were embedded in the People's Budget of 29th April 1909. It had been a centuries-old convention that the Lords could not reject or even modify a money bill; for the Upper House to withold funds needed for the carrying on of the government of the country was, Asquith said, a 'usurpation of the rights of the Commons'. It was generally believed that the inclusion of fresh and sweeping reforms in Lloyd George's first Budget was merely an attempt to get them through the Lords: some regarded it as chicanery, a knavish conspiracy devised by Lloyd George and Churchill. But Lloyd George said it was done because funds were required for the reforms. On Budget Day these two men, Churchill and Lloyd George, walked from the Treasury to the House of Commons together. Lloyd George told the House bluntly that he was resolved on 'robbing the hen roosts'. In a rousing peroration he said: 'This is a War Budget. It is for raising money to wage war against poverty and squalidness. I cannot help believing that before this generation has passed away, we shall have advanced a great step towards that good time when poverty, wretchedness and the human degradation which always followed in its camp will be as remote to the people of this country as the wolves which once infested its forests.'

Chief of these reforms was the introduction of national insurance against ill health (this brought in the panel doctors) and insurance against unemployment. Old age pensions were increased. To raise money a tax was put on motorcars and on petrol—by 1909 the motor-car was increasingly in evidence even in the towns, but it was still the old upright contraption, looking very like a coachman's dickey-box, with a sort of wide sedan chair behind it, containing two or four seats. Income tax was raised from a shilling in the pound to one and twopence: family allowances were introduced for the first time and the rate for unearned income was made higher than for earned. A supertax was also imposed, though no more than a mere twopence in the pound. But the new death duties were crushing: they were increased by 33⅓ per cent. Two new methods of taxing land were proposed: unearned increases in land values, as well as a tax on undeveloped land. All the land in the country was valued to provide a basis for taxation.

The Lords rejected the Budget. The King had tried hard to prevent this. The last thing he wanted was a head-on collision between the two Houses. Already on two occasions he had tried to act as mediator—on the Education Bill and on the Licensing Bill. He strove now to work out a compromise in the Budget conflict. One suggestion he made was to strengthen the Government's position in the Upper House, not by creating a vast horde of new hereditary Liberal peers but by raising to the peerage the eldest sons of Liberal peers (this would have doubled their number, which being only seventy-five would not, however, have been enough) and further, by introducing something completely new, namely life peerages, to add to that total a sufficient number to get the Budget through. But Asquith rejected this.

The Conservatives meanwhile mustered every available peer. Most of them had never taken any interest in politics, many hadn't even troubled to take the oath. They came up to London from their country seats—they were called 'backwoodsmen'—were sworn in and trooped into the lobbies to register their votes. The Budget was defeated by 350 votes to 75, the largest majority against any Government since Gladstone's Home Rule Bill of 1886.

It was inevitable now that a final battle would have to be fought to resolve the *impasse*. Lloyd George's attacks rose to a climax. 'It will be asked,' he said at Newcastle, 'why 500 ordinary men, chosen accidentally from among the unemployed, should override the judgment—the deliberate judgment—of millions of people.' And at Wolverhampton he said this of the Lords: 'No testimonials are required. There are no credentials. They do not even need a medical certificate. They need not be sound, either in body or in mind. They only require a certificate of birth, just to prove that they are the first of the litter. You would not choose a spaniel on these principles.'

Asquith decided to appeal to the country. He wanted the voters to give the Government a mandate to settle the dispute. He was confident of winning. The election campaign was opened at the Albert Hall where ten thousand people had assembled, but all women were excluded because only a few weeks before some suffragettes had dog-whipped Winston Churchill at Bristol. 'The will of the people,' Asquith said, 'as deliberately expressed by their elected representatives, must, within the lifetime of a single Parliament, be made to prevail.' The powers of the Upper House would have to be curtailed if this was to be achieved. In future it would only be possible for them to reject Bills that had already been passed by the Commons for two sessions and no more—after that the Bills would be passed automatically.

Asquith, it was believed, had obtained a promise from the King that, if the Liberals won, he would create enough peers to get the Budget through. The King had in fact refused to agree to this. Asquith's secretary has recorded his talk with the King's secretary: 'The King had come to the conclusion that he would not be justified in creating new peers (say 300) until after a second General Election.'[31]

The Conservatives were equally confident of winning. The result actually was in effect a draw—the Liberals lost a great many seats and had a majority of only two over their opponents, getting 275 votes to 273; but they could of course count on the 82 Irish Nationalists and the 40 Labour members to force almost any Bill through the House of Commons.

Not unnaturally the Tories declared the verdict to be inconclusive. The Government had not been given a clear mandate to deal decisively with the House of Lords. The King was of the same opinion. He told Haldane, who was a personal friend, that he could not possibly consider the creation of peers without a much more definite expression of opinion from the country. 'As I was taking my leave,' Haldane adds in his diary,[32] 'he said "This Government may not last." '

His Majesty was too disturbed about the position to leave it at that. His mind still sought a solution. A week after the election, Crewe, the Liberal Leader of the Lords, was invited to Windsor to be one of a small party of men. After dinner the King had a long talk alone with him about the future of the Upper House and put forward still another solution. He suggested that while no peer should be debarred from attending and taking part in the debates, the voting should be confined to no more than one hundred peers, each Party selecting half that number. He realised that the numbers being equal there might be a deadlock, but was convinced that in the Lords, where there were many independent and moderate-minded men, every effort would be made to avoid a collision with the Commons and important Government measures would be dealt with in a spirit of compromise. Lord Crewe pointed out a danger that the King had not foreseen. What if each leader, he said, selected fifty men whom they could count on to support the Party through thick and thin. His Majesty accepted that that was possible.

Both sides would, for example, leave out the Archbishop of Canterbury, because they could not be certain of getting his vote. He asked Crewe to think of some other way out and promised to give it a great deal of further anxious thought himself.

The Prime Minister, however, had by no means abandoned the idea of creating further peers. There was the Budget to get through. Nine months had passed since its rejection by the Lords and this was seriously affecting the conduct of the financial business of the country. Noticing the King's uneasiness when he was told this, Asquith assured His Majesty that he would not ask for the creation of additional peers unless the situation became critical. The King's uneasiness grew. He at once had a word with the Leader of the Tory Opposition and wrote to Asquith: 'I find that the Opposition will probably vote against the Government on the Budget, in consequence of the attitude which they took up, both in Parliament and at the Election, in regard to certain points of that measure. I understand, however, that it is not the wish of the Opposition to throw unnecessary obstacles in the way of the Government business which is connected with finance.' This meant that the Tories wanted the reforms to be separated from the Budget. Asquith was not prepared to agree to that.

The King had been markedly cool of late in his manner towards the Prime Minister and Asquith feared that he might show his displeasure by refusing to open Parliament on 22nd February 1910. The King's reply, when told this, was brief and blunt: 'It is at present my full intention of opening Parliament with the Queen, as I have done on all previous occasions since my accession to the Throne.' When he received the Speech from the Throne, His Majesty was very critical and made a great many alterations. In its final form the revised paragraphs read: 'You will be asked to complete the provision which was made in the last session of Parliament for the year about to expire, but to which effect has not yet been given. The expenditure authorised by the last Parliament is being duly incurred, but as the reserve required to meet it has not yet been provided by the imposition of taxation, recourse has been had, under Parliamentary sanction, to temporary borrowing. Arrangements must be made at the earliest possible moment to deal with the financial situation thus created.

'My Lords and Gentlemen—Recent experience has disclosed serious difficulties due to recurring differences of strong opinion between the two branches of the Legislature. Proposals will be laid before you, with all convenient speed, to define the relations between the Houses of Parliament, so as to secure the undivided authority of the House of Commons over Finance, and its predominance over Legislation. The measures, in the opinion of my advisers, should provide that this House (of Lords) should be so constituted and empowered as to exercise impartially in regard to proposed Legislation the functions of initiation, revision and, subject to proper safeguards, of delay.'

Asquith had said before the election that the Government would 'not hold office unless we can secure the safeguards'. He found it necessary now to explain in the Commons, in view of the rumours that had been sweeping the country, that no promise had been obtained from the King for the creation of additional peers and that it would have been improper to ask for it. This immediately angered the Irish: they were anxious to curb the power of the Lords who were against Home Rule. The Irish leader accordingly informed the Prime Minister that, unless the removal of the Lords veto became law 'this year', they were not prepared to support the Government on the Budget. The Cabinet, well aware that they were dependent on the Irish vote, discussed the threat and later Asquith informed the King that many were of the opinion that the Government should resign. Asquith added, however, that he did not share that view and had informed the Irish members that he would give no assurances and that they must act as they pleased.

The Government was in an extremely precarious position. The Irish did not like the Budget and had already voted against it in the previous Parliament and if they did so again the Government would certainly fall. But Asquith worked out a surprisingly effective way round it. He introduced not Bills but a series of resolutions, setting down the principles for reforming the Lords. This brought him the support of the Irish. Next he introduced a Finance Bill to carry the 1909 Budget into law. The Irish supported this too, and when it was sent up to the Lords it was passed by them in a single sitting. Thus was Lloyd George's famous People's Budget at last got through.

The Parliament Bill to curb the vote of the Lords was the next measure. While this was being prepared the King died. An inevitable delay followed, for Asquith was considerate enough to feel that the new King, George the Fifth, should be given enough time to get his bearings. Meanwhile he decided to have a second General Election. But before going to the country he asked for and, despite His Majesty's utmost reluctance, he succeeded in extracting the promise that hundreds of new peers would be created if necessary.

In this second election in 1910 the Government lost five seats, the Tories won twenty, but the great increase in the number of Labour and Irish Members made the Government's position very much as before. The Parliament Bill was sent to their lordships in the following January. It was mauled mercilessly. About a hundred peers, who came to be known as 'Diehards', were prepared to 'die in the ditch' rather than surrender. But on learning of the pledge given by the King, Lansdowne, Leader of the Tories in the Lords, tried desperately to persuade the Diehards to be conciliatory. He succeeded. The Bill scraped through with a majority of 17: in addition to the by now 81 Liberal peers, 37 Tory peers and 13 bishops voted for it. The power of the Upper House was finally curbed.

CHAPTER 22

The Changes Sweep In

Change is often imperceptible. It crept in during Victoria's long reign, but the overall impress of Her Majesty continued to colour the era to the end. The Edwardian age spanned barely a decade, but the brisk flow of the many varied inventions made the process of change much more rapid; only the stamp of Edward's forceful personality maintained an apparent uniformity throughout those years, but the scene had almost completely altered by the time of his death. A fading flicker lingered, but shortly after his passing it vanished.

Signs that the King's health was failing became evident early in 1909. He was never prepared to admit, even to himself, that he was not perfectly fit. He loathed being ill and it was only with the utmost difficulty that the doctors could persuade him to stay in bed. His constitution in fact had never been robust. At the age of thirty he was not expected to live. He got typhoid while staying with friends near Scarborough and a fellow guest, also infected it was believed by the foul drains, died a few days later. By a strange coincidence Edward's father, Prince Albert, had died of typhoid exactly ten years before and a feeling of impending doom hung over Sandringham when the Court physicians pronounced Edward's condition to be desperate. Queen Victoria hurried to his bedside and slept on a mattress on the floor of Princess Alexandra's bedroom alongside. On the evening of 11th December she was told that the end must be expected during the night. The Prince raved for thirty-six hours, talking, singing, whistling, but though he gasped for breath, he managed to cling on to life. The crisis came on the 14th, the exact anniversary of his father's death. But by the evening the fever left him and slowly he began to recover. Again, at the time of his postponed Coronation, he was not expected to survive the operation for appendicitis.

During the latter part of his life he suffered recurrently from bronchitis. It returned every year in February. His excessive weight was not conducive to good health and his annual visit to Homburg and later Marienbad to drink the waters did little to correct the damage done by his unremitting indulgence in enormous meals, of which Queen Alexandra complained constantly. He smoked cigars endlessly and was often short of breath. On 8th February 1909, when he set out with the Queen on a State visit to Berlin immediately after a bout of bronchitis, he appeared to be weak and ailing, but refused to abandon the arranged schedule. The Kaiser and Kaiserin met them at the railway station, and Lord Grenfell, who was a member of the King's party, records that there was 'a great deal of embracing between the royalties'.[26] The route to the Palace was lined by the Imperial Guard, 20,000 of them counting cavalry and infantry.

The King's fatigue was very marked at the banquet that evening. Instead of replying to the toast with an extempore speech, as was his custom, he read out the speech. He looked tired and coughed constantly. The next day he had a crowded programme of lunch, dinner and civic receptions. At the opera that night he fell asleep and woke up with a start to find the stage on fire. There were tongues of flame and great billowing clouds of smoke, and the King wondered why the firemen in the wings were making no effort to put the fire out. But the Kaiserin reassured him that it was merely a very realistic presentation of the last scene and there was no danger whatsoever. After the performance he felt unable to go round and talk to the cast, so Queen Alexandra went instead and did it superbly, talking all the time without hearing a word anyone said.

The next day, after a big lunch at the British Embassy, he had a severe fit of coughing and collapsed. There was instant alarm. The room was quickly emptied. Doctors were brought in. The attack passed and the King, with complete disregard, helped himself to another large cigar and resumed his conversation with the Ambassador and the guests. The Controller of the Kaiser's Household, Count Zedlitz-Trüstzschler, who was present, records:[35] 'The King of England is so stout that he completely loses his breath when he has to climb upstairs, and has to save himself in many ways. The Emperor told us that at the first family dinner he fell asleep. At the lunch at the British Embassy he was indisposed for a few minutes, but he eats, drinks, and smokes enormously.' Still in evidence, however, was His Majesty's amiable manner and his clear and vigorous memory. The Controller added: He 'takes a hand when there is something of special importance to call for his intervention, and then with his age and experience and thorough knowledge of the world he acts very adroitly. I can imagine that a sly and amiable smile steals over his face when he thinks how the whole world looks upon him as the guiding spirit of all the solid and brilliant achievements of British diplomacy.'

This was in fact the King's first official visit to Berlin since his accession eight years before; and although he carried it through despite his failing health, the bitterness of the winter, and at considerable physical strain to himself, critics in the German Press were not slow to point out that he had in the intervening years visited not only Paris many times, and Rome and Vienna, but also such lesser capitals as Brussels, Lisbon and Copenhagen. They omitted, however, to mention that the King had offered to come on a State visit to Berlin in 1904 but had been brusquely put off by the Kaiser. Daisy, Princess of Pless, has left a vivid vignette of the Kaiser. 'Take him as a man he is impossible, he has no manners.' She supplies an illustration of this. She saw him

Above: The Thunderbolt of
War

Below: The Impudent Albion
(*Jean Veber, copyright by*
Spadem, *Paris, 1964*)

in the distance one night during a ball at Potsdam and 'made him a little bow from the other end of the room. He beckoned to me, calling me with his finger and then pointing to the floor. At first I did not move, refusing to believe his manner which was as if he was calling a naughty child to come and stand before him. But at the third time I had to go.'[50]

King Edward returned to London for the opening of Parliament in February and left shortly afterwards for Biarritz to enjoy the sunshine. When he came back two months later, instead of looking refreshed and tanned, his face had a startling pallor and he seemed to have aged greatly. But he could not be deterred from carrying on with his usual round of duties—official dinners and receptions, interviews with Ministers, the endless flow of State documents, and numerous other public activities.

In the summer his health improved and after winning the Derby, for the third time, with Minoru, he was at the top of his form. Cowes followed and with it came the visit of the Tsar and Tsaritsa of Russia and the five-year-old Tsarevitch who was King Edward's godson. The King sent three of the largest battleships to escort the Tsar's yacht and set out himself in the *Victoria and Albert* to welcome him as he entered the Solent. The British fleet was there in massive strength—24 battleships, 16 armoured cruisers, 48 destroyers and more than 50 other vessels of war. Never before had Britannia's might been so impressively assembled. Soon it was to be even stronger. Persistent rumours about Germany's naval expansion presented a challenge that had to be met. To begin with Britain planned to build four new dreadnoughts. This was raised now to six—the Tories demanded eight, and the music-halls took up the refrain 'We want eight and we won't wait!' Lloyd George and Churchill refused to yield on this, but Sir Edward Grey threatened to resign unless they did and eight was finally agreed to.

The rivalry between Britain and Germany went on unabated. Some heard the distant rumble of war, which they regarded as inevitable and inescapable. Its prospect disturbed Edward too. All through his reign he had been seeking through alliances some way to avert it. In January 1910, a few weeks before his death, he tried still again. Writing to the Kaiser for his birthday he included in his greeting these words: 'It is essential for the peace of the world that we should walk shoulder to shoulder for the good of civilisation and the prosperity of the world.' The Kaiser, replying to his 'Dearest Uncle,' declared that that 'has always been the leading maxim of my policy,' and spoke of 'the mischief which is being wrought by an unscrupulous Press lamentably deficient in veracity, prompted by greed for sensations. But I feel convinced,' he went on, 'that the main body of sensible people in the countries will remain unmoved and help to maintain the feelings of friendship and good will and to strengthen the ties between them.'[5] Unfortunately it was otherwise.

Soon the King's health began to cause his doctors some anxiety. Violent fits of coughing had developed and at times he appeared to be choking. They urged him to leave London as quickly as possible. The purer oxygen of Biarritz, they said, would do him a lot of good. But the King refused to go because of the political crisis over the future of the House of Lords which had now reached its acutest form. 'If he had been a private individual,' one of his doctors said, 'we should have had him away long ago. We know how serious his condition is.' Asquith added his voice to the doctors' and a temporary lull in the crisis led to his agreeing to go. At a large dinner at Buckingham Palace on the night before he left, despite his cheerfulness and his gay conversation, many noticed that the strain of overwork had begun to tell. He broke the journey in Paris, went to the theatre on both nights, and caught a cold which got worse by the time he reached Biarritz and developed into a prolonged attack of bronchitis. He went on working at the State papers that kept arriving from London, much to the alarm of his doctor who saw that his heart was no longer able to take the strain of his violent spasms of coughing.

The King was away in all for seven weeks. Within an hour

or so of returning to London, although extremely tired, he insisted on dressing and going to the opera. He was busy all the next day seeing Ministers and talking to the United States Ambassador about President Theodore Roosevelt's visit to London in two weeks. Two nights later he went to see *Siegfried* at Covent Garden, then left for Sandringham for the week-end, but on Monday, 2nd May, he was back in town. Queen Alexandra was at the time in Greece, and had urged him to join her there for a cruise, but he felt he couldn't go too far away because of the Lords crisis. She promptly left Corfu and hurried home. Unabatedly the work went on as well as endless audiences. When urged to rest he brushed the advice aside. 'No, I shall not give in. I shall work to the end. Of what use is it to be alive if one cannot work.' He went to the Royal Academy, visited Mrs Alice Keppel to play cards, the next day she came and had tea with him. It was on the evening of the Queen's return, Thursday, 5th May, that a medical bulletin stated that the King had bronchitis and his condition was causing some anxiety.

He rose early the next morning and insisted on dressing. His voice was feeble. When Sir Ernest Cassel arrived at noon His Majesty lit a cigar, but after a while he collapsed. Nevertheless he refused to go to bed. After a light lunch in his bedroom, his nurses helped him into a chair. A series of heart attacks followed. The doctors abandoned hope and the Archbishop of Canterbury was sent for. All through that afternoon at Queen Alexandra's wish, Mrs Alice Keppel and others of his closest and dearest friends, came to see him, entering the room one by one. But all attempts to help him to his bed were resisted. His heir informed him at 5 o'clock that his horse had won the Two-Year-Old Plate at Kempton Park. 'I am very glad,' King Edward said. Later that evening he died. He was sixty-eight. Thus the Edwardian Age may be said to have ended at 11.45 p.m. on Friday, 6th May 1910.

King George the Fifth wrote briefly but movingly in his diary: 'I have lost my best friend and the best of fathers. I never had a word with him in my life. I am heartbroken and overwhelmed with grief.' No father and son have ever been closer. Edward was devoted to his children—to all children: he had himself suffered in childhood and tried to give to others what he had missed and had yearned for. His grandson, the Duke of Windsor, writes: 'If the superimposition of four noisy children upon the Royal Household during my parents' absence was ever a nuisance, my grandparents never let us know it. On the contrary, they encouraged our innate boisterousness to such an extent that the quiet routine of York Cottage suffered a brief but harmless setback .... If my grandparents were not entertaining distinguished company at lunch, they liked to have us romping around in the dining-room. In this congenial atmosphere it was easy to forget that Mlle Bricka was waiting for us upstairs with her French and German primers. If we were too long in going, she would enter the dining-room timidly to warn us that we were already late for our afternoon lessons. Usually my grandmother would wave her away, and my grandfather, puffing at his cigar, might add reassuringly to the governess, "It's all right. Let the children stay with us a little longer. We shall send them upstairs presently." '[68]

Mrs Keppel's daughter Sonia writes of the King: 'In my life, Kingy filled the place of an accepted, kind uncle, of whom I was much less in awe than I was of my Uncle Harry, Major of the Tower of London. . . . Kingy's advent had always meant fun to me. Even if sometimes I saw him in uniform, it was always on an occasion of public rejoicing.' Of his death she says: 'Inside our house, fear of Kingy's health muted each voice, and, for the first time, I was afraid to approach my stern, unsmiling mother. My father was easier but he, too, was absorbed and serious. . . . The day wore on and the routine of it did nothing to alleviate my fear. I had no idea what I was afraid of, but, at every moment, I was aware of it.' She was put to bed at the end of the day and learned next morning that Kingy was dead. 'At a few minutes notice, Papa and Mamma had left the house overnight, and were now with Mrs Arthur James in Grafton Street.' The child was taken there by her Nannie.

'A pall of darkness hung over the house,' she writes. 'Blinds were drawn, lights were dimmed, and black clothes appeared, even for me, with black ribbons threaded through my underclothes. . . . We were told Mamma was in bed and when we were escorted to her room, Mrs James barred our way.' Nevertheless she and her sister Violet went in. 'We went up to her bed and she turned and looked at us blankly, and without recognition, and rather resentfully, as though we were unwelcome intruders. . . . Kingy's death,' she adds, 'had changed all our lives.' Going to her father for comfort, she was told simply: 'Nothing will ever be quite the same again.'

That was the feeling throughout the country. Nothing was quite the same again. In every home every blind was drawn that day. Through the main streets of Coulsdon when a motor-cycle tore by, women rushed to their front doors, shocked that anyone should disturb the silence of that day by making so much noise.

That strident, shattering note, increasing in volume in the streets and in the skies, was to destroy finally the quiet and calm of an age which those old enough to remember it recall with a nostalgic sigh. It replaced the gentle tinkle of the muffin bell and the melodious song of the gipsies selling 'sweet-smelling lavender'. More silently but with as marked an emphasis, taxes soared, the cost of food rose and women took on startling new roles: their stately elegance began to fade, their long sweeping skirts vanished, their whaleboned figures assumed fresh shapes and men abandoned their high choker collars. In the distance the sharp ears of the discerning could hear the faint, unmistakable thunder of war. It came. Soon men-about-town, playboys, youths at the cricket nets, clerks in offices and banks were no longer to be seen in the streets. And when the lights were dimmed and the blinds were drawn to observe the black-out it was like sounding the 'Last Post' at the passing of a cherished Age.

Acknowledgments

I have based my portrait of the Edwardian Age partly on childhood memories, amply elaborated by older relatives and friends. I have also drawn on *The Times* and a number of other newspapers and on magazines such as *Punch*, *Illustrated London News*, *Sphere*, *Tatler* and the *Queen*. The books referred to are listed in the Bibliography.

My thanks are also due to Bertrand Russell, Mrs Roland Cubitt (Mrs Keppel's daughter Sonia), Sir John Elliot, Miles Malleson, James Laver and many retired restaurateurs, waiters, Savile Row tailors and dress-designers who have given unstintingly of their time to help me.

Bibliography

1 *Recollections of Three Reigns*, Sir Frederick Ponsonby, first Lord Sysonby (Eyre & Spottiswoode 1951).
2 *King Edward the Seventh, An Appreciation*, E. F. Benson (Longmans, Green 1933).
3 *Edwardian England, 1901-1910*, edited F. J. C. Hearnshaw (Benn 1933).
4 *King Edward and His Times*, André Maurois (Cassell 1933).
5 *King Edward the Seventh*, A biography, 2 volumes, Sir Sidney Lee (Macmillan 1927).
6 *Daughters of Queen Victoria*, E. F. Benson (Cassell 1939)
7 *The Delightful Profession: Edward VII. A Study in Kingship*, H. E. Wortham (Cape 1931).
8 *Edward VII and His Circle*, Virginia Cowles (Hamish Hamilton 1956).
9 *The Fabulous Leonard Jerome*, Anita Leslie (Hutchinson 1954).
10 *Lord Randolph Churchill*, Rt. Hon. Winston Spencer Churchill, M.P. (Macmillan 1907).
11 *King Edward as a Sportsman*, Alfred E. T. Watson (Longmans, Green 1911).
12 *As We Were. A Victorian Peepshow*, E. F. Benson (Longmans, Green 1930).
13 *The British Monarchy at Home*, J. A. Frere (Anthony Gibbs 1963).
14 *The Days I Knew*, Lillie Langtry, Lady de Bathe (Hutchinson 1925).
15 *More Memories*, Margot Asquith, Countess of Oxford and Asquith (Cassell 1933).
16 *King Edward VII*, Lord Redesdale (Valentine Press 1915).

17 *King Edward VII and His Court: Some Reminiscences*, Sir Lionel Cust, K.C.V.O. (Murray 1930).

18 *Rosebery*, Robert Rhodes James (Weidenfeld & Nicolson 1963).

19 *The Diary of Lady Frederick Cavendish* (John Murray 1922).

20 *Journals and Letters of Reginald*, 4 volumes, Viscount Esher (Nicholson & Watson 1939).

21 *Memoirs*, Prince Christopher of Greece (Hurst & Blackett 1938).

22 *King Edward VII, Biographical and Personal Memoirs*, Bella Sidney Woolf and others (Skeffington 1910).

23 *England under Edward VII*, J. A. Farrer (Allen & Unwin 1922).

24 *Ten Years in the Court of St. James'*, Baron Herman von Eckardstein (Butterworth 1921).

25 *Philip, Count Eulenburg*, 2 volumes. Head of the Kaiser's Household. (Secker 1930).

26 *Memoirs of Lord Grenfell* (Hodder & Stoughton 1925).

27 *The Life of the Rt. Hon. Sir Henry Campbell-Bannerman*, 2 volumes, J. A. Spender (Hodder & Stoughton 1923).

28 *My Early Life*, Winston S. Churchill (Thornton Butterworth 1930).

29 *Life and Letters*, 2 volumes, Rt. Hon. George Wyndham (Hutchinson 1925).

30 *The Marquess of Lincolnshire's Diary* (Documents in possession of Brigader A. W. P. Llewellen Palmer).

31 *Herbert Henry Asquith*, 2 volumes, J. A. Spender and Cyril Asquith (Hutchinson 1932).

32 *Haldane, 1856-1928. The Life of Viscount Haldane of Cloan*, 2 volumes, Sir Frederick Maurice (Faber & Faber 1937-9).

33 *British Documents on the Origin of the War*, edited G. P. Gooch and Harold Timperley, Vol. III (Stationery Office 1928).

34 *Queen Alexandra*, Sir George Arthur (Chapman & Hall 1934).

35 *Twelve Years at the German Court*, R. V. Zedlitz-Trüstzschler (Nisbet 1924).

36 *The Day Before Yesterday*, edited Noel Streatfeild (Collins 1956).

37 *Things Past*, Duchess of Sermoneta (Hutchinson 1929).

38 *Life and Labour of the People in London*, 9 volumes, Charles Booth (Macmillan N.Y. 1892/97).

39 *My Apprenticeship*, Beatrice Webb (Longmans, Green 1926).

40 *Democracy and Reaction*, L. T. Hobhouse (Unwin 1904).

41 *R.D.B's Diary 1887-1914*, R. D. Blumenfeld (Heinemann 1930).

42 *The Cause*, Ray Strachey (Bell 1928).

43 *Votes for Women*, Roger Fulford (Faber & Faber 1957).

44 *King Edward the Seventh*, Sir Philip Magnus (John Murray 1964).

45 *Embassies of Other Days*, 2 volumes, Walburga, Lady Paget (Hutchinson 1923).

46 *The Letters of Queen Victoria*, 3 volumes, edited A. C. Benson and Viscount Esher (Murray 1907).

47 *The Memoirs of an Ex-Minister*, Lord Malmesbury (Longmans, Green 1884).

48 *The Private Life of Queen Alexandra*, Hans Roger Madol (Hutchinson 1940).

49 *A Century of Fashion*, J. P. Worth (Little 1928).

50 *Daisy, Princess of Pless* by Herself (John Murray 1928).

51 *Kitchener: Portrait of an Imperialist*, Philip Magnus (John Murray 1958).

52 *Memoirs, 1839-1916*, Lord Sandwich, edited Mrs Stewart Erskine (Murray 1919).

53 *All in a Lifetime*, R. D. Blumenfeld (Benn 1931).

54 *The Gilded Lily*, Ernest Dudley (Odhams 1958).

55 *Afterthoughts*, Frances, Countess of Warwick (Cassell 1931).

56 *Edwardian Daughter*, Sonia Keppel (Hamish Hamilton 1958).

57 *Memoirs*, 3 volumes, Prince von Bülow (Putnam 1931).

58 *The Autobiography of Margot Asquith*, 2 volumes. (Butterworth 1920-2).

59 *Edwardian Hey-Days*, George Cornwallis-West (Putnam 1930).

60 *Famous Illnesses in History*, R. Scott Stevenson, M.D., F.R.C.S. (Eyre & Spottiswoode 1962).

61 *Royal Chef*, Gabriel Tschumi (Kimber 1954).

62 *Four Studies in Loyalty*, Christopher Sykes (Collins 1946).

63 *Life's Ebb and Flow*, Frances, Countess of Warwick (Hutchinson 1929).

64 *Eighteen Years on Sandringham Estate*, 'The Lady Farmer' (Privately printed).

65 *The Whole Art of Dining*, J. Rey (Carmona & Baker 1920).

66 *Grand Deception*, edited Alexander Klein (Faber & Faber 1956).

67 *My Diaries*, Wilfred Scawen Blunt, Vol. 2, 1900-1914 (Martin Secker 1920).

68 *A King's Story, The Memoirs of H.R.H. the Duke of Windsor* (Cassell 1951).

69 *Dinners and Diners*, Col. Newnham-Davis (Richards 1904).

70 *Taste and Fashion: From the French Revolution to the Present Day,* James Laver (Harrap 1945).

71 *Edward VII and Queen Alexandra. A Biography in Word and Picture*, Helmut and Alison Gernsheim (Muller 1962).

72 *Queen Victoria. A Biography in Word and Picture*, Helmut and Alison Gernsheim (Muller 1959).

73 *What I have Left Unsaid*, Daisy, Princess of Pless (Cassell 1936).

74 *Aviation*, Aljernon E. Berriman (Methuen 1913).

75 *Bismarck: The Man and the Statesman*, A. J. P. Taylor (Hamish Hamilton 1955).

76 *Arthur James Balfour*, Kenneth Young (Bell 1963).

77 *Old Pink 'Un Days*, J. B. Borth (Grant Richards 1924).

78 *A Pink 'Un and a Pelican: Some Random Reminiscences, Sporting and Otherwise*, Arthur M. Binstead and Ernest Wells (Bliss, Sands 1898).

79 *The Glass of Fashion*, Cecil Beaton (Weidenfeld & Nicolson 1954).

80 *The Art of Fine Living*, André Simon (Michael Joseph 1929).

81 *Life's Enchanted Cup*, Mrs C. S. Peel (Bodley Head 1933).

82 *Society in the New Reign*, A Foreign Resident (Unwin 1904).

Index